Coming Off Drink

James Ditzler is a psychologist who trained in chemical dependence at the internationally renowned Hazelden Foundation in Minnesota and later worked at the Roosevelt Hospital in New York. Since 1975 he has been treating addicts and alcoholics in Britain.

Joyce Ditzler is a state-registered nurse, trained at Guy's Hospital, London. She trained in addiction at the Roosevelt Hospital in New York. She has been treating addicts and alcoholics in Britain since 1975.

Farm Place, which was founded and is run by James and Joyce Ditzler, is a residential treatment centre for addicts and alcoholics, with high success rates.

Maurice Lipsedge is a consultant psychiatrist with an interest in alcoholism and addiction.

James Ditzler, MA, Sp.D.Psych.,
and Joyce Ditzler, SRN, RN

Coming Off Drink

PAPERMAC

To Clint and Marie

First published 1987 by
PAPERMAC
a division of Macmillan Publishers Limited
4 Little Essex Street London WC2R 3LF
and Basingstoke

Associated companies in Auckland, Delhi, Dublin, Gaborone,
Hamburg, Harare, Hong Kong, Johannesburg, Kuala Lumpur,
Lagos, Manzini, Melbourne, Mexico City, Nairobi, New York,
Singapore and Tokyo

British Library Cataloguing in Publication Data
Ditzler, James
    Coming off drink.
    1.   Alcoholism —— Treatment
    I.   Title   II. Ditzler, Joyce
    362.2'92   RC565

    ISBN 0-333-44673-9
    ISBN 0-333-44480-9 Pbk

Typeset by Columns of Reading
Printed in Great Britain by Anchor Brendon Ltd., Tiptree, Essex

Contents

Acknowledgements

To the staff of Farm Place for their encouragement; to Eve Ling for her patient typing of the manuscript; to Celia Haddon for her continuing help and encouragement; and to all ex-patients and the members of the Twelve-Step programmes whose experience of recovery, shared, has been our inspiration through the years.

Introduction

Recent public concern about the use of illicit drugs has diverted attention from the less sensational but far more widespread damage caused by excessive drinking. In the United Kingdom, per capita average consumption rose by 87 per cent between 1950 and 1976, with a corresponding increase in deaths from cirrhosis of the liver, and in admissions to mental hospital for alcoholism. In an average general practice population of 2500 patients, about twenty will have a serious drinking problem, while between one-tenth and one-quarter of patients in general hospital medical wards have alcohol-induced physical disorders. Alcohol-related problems include not only physical and mental ill-health, but also a significant proportion of road-traffic and industrial accidents, and of violent crime. One-third of divorcees killed in road-traffic accidents have an excessive amount of alcohol in their blood, while 50 per cent of battered wives report that their husbands indulge in frequent heavy drinking. The rate of absenteeism among alcoholics is between two and four times greater than in the general population. Nearly half of the murderers in Britain have been drinking before committing their offence, while up to one in ten of hospitalised alcoholics eventually commit suicide.

The Ditzlers draw attention to women as problem drinkers. While survey data shows that men continue to constitute both the majority of heavy drinkers and a higher percentage of physical and social problems, over the past decade there has been a significant increase in alcohol-related problems among women, especially women aged between twenty and thirty. The old stereotype of the woman alcoholic as the middle-aged suburban housewife has to be reviewed since working women seem to be overtaking housewives as potential problem drinkers.

The authors regard alcoholism as a disease. Although this has the advantage of distinguishing alcoholics and protecting them from the charge of moral degeneracy and absolving them from guilt, the disease label is regarded as inappropriate by most physicians, because although everybody agrees that chronic alcohol abuse can cause physical damage, the same might be said of a number of other self-destructive activities, such as over-eating or promiscuity. It might be helpful for the sceptical reader to substitute the word 'vulnerability' for 'disease', since this term implies an underlying susceptibility to dependence on mood-altering substances (including not only alcohol but also tranquillisers and sleeping pills) and emphasises the life-long risk of relapse.

Alcoholism as a disorder affecting every member of the heavy-drinking individual's family rightly receives a great deal of attention in this book. The authors demonstrate the role of denial in both the drinkers' attitudes and behaviour, and in their spouses' and children's. Communication with the families of alcoholics tends to become destructive, while alcohol abuse can act as a 'disavowel' technique which allows the norms of acceptable behaviour to be disregarded. Young children in a family affected by alcoholism are sometimes forced prematurely into adult roles and have to care for their own parents while being emotionally, and at times physically, neglected. In addition to the problems of emotional neglect and physical abuse, the alcoholic parent's behaviour is inconsistent and unpredictable while the non-alcoholic parent is perceived as ineffectual and helpless. Both parents present confusing models of mature behaviour and children may learn to survive by relying on techniques which are inappropriate in adult life, such as being over-placatory or taking on a nursing role.

The Ditzlers give valuable practical advice on how to deal with craving and on how to cope with social situations in the early stages of recovery when there is outside pressure to take a drink. They give a timely warning on the risks of substituting a dependence on tranquillisers for addiction to alcohol. The families of alcoholics are counselled to avoid self-blame, and are warned against assuming responsibility for the alcoholic and against over-protecting him or her. The futility of threatening, lecturing, hectoring and nagging is underlined, and both alcoholics and their families are advised against fruitless searching for 'underlying reasons' for problem drinking. As in their approach to drug addiction, the critical therapeutic ingredient is confronting alcoholics with the damaging consequences of dependence and getting them to take responsibility for their own behaviour.

The Ditzlers strongly advocate Alcoholics Anonymous and Al-Anon. These organisations help foster a frank sharing of experience and an exchange of practical strategies for coping with common problems. The warmly welcoming, accepting and unthreatening atmosphere of meetings provides participants with support and emotional sustenance, which are valuable correctives to the damage to self-esteem resulting from the years of isolated remorse generated by chronic or recurrent heavy drinking, or by having to cope with this behaviour in a spouse or parent. The Alcoholics Anonymous emphasis on total abstinence as the only viable long-term goal applies to the majority of alcoholics and, since it is impossible to predict which individuals might be able to stick to 'sensible' drinking, an abstinence-based programme such as that recommended by the Ditzlers seems at present to be the most practical.

Maurice Lipsedge

PART ONE

The Road to Recovery

1

How Alcoholics Recover

Alcoholism is a disease, not a disgrace. Alcoholics are sick people who need to get well, not bad people who need to be good. And they can and do get well when they come off and stay off drink. Thousands of alcoholics have proved this for themselves. No matter how severe their illness, they have managed to come off drink and stay off it. They are now leading normal and happy lives.

Alcoholism is a treatable illness, not a moral issue, and since 1969 we have been treating alcoholics, both as in-patients and as out-patients, and we have seen literally thousands of them recover. Our former patients include all kinds of men and women, and by now many of them have been off drink for up to seventeen years.

We know it can be done. If you are an alcoholic, you can do it too. If you are the parents, partner or child of one, take heart – your loved one can do it.

Here is the story of just one of those alcoholics we know who is now off drink, and leading a happy and useful life.

Lucy's story

Lucy drank from the age of thirteen. She discovered that she liked alcohol at one of her parent's parties, when she nipped down to see the fun and slipped from one room to another drinking out of other people's glasses. 'Very soon', she says, 'I felt wonderful, quite different from how I had ever felt before. It was like a whole new world.'

Her mother spotted her and sent her off to bed but Lucy didn't forget that feeling. She continued her normal life at home and at school, and gradually started going to parties herself. She liked to drink and thought it was very grown up and smart.

At fifteen she went to a disco with a girlfriend. They soon met a crowd of friends and they were all drinking. Lucy became very impatient with them – they got silly on so little.

At seventeen she was asked to leave school after several warnings about her behaviour. She had become very rebellious and restless, always needing to be the centre of attention. She took pot into school and that – after several instances when she had missed school because of her drinking – was the last straw for her teachers. But they did not know that she was now drinking regularly, stealing from her parents' drinks cupboard, from supermarkets and even from friends' houses.

'I thought it was just a giggle,' said Lucy, but it was soon to become less funny. 'I was coming home from the pub one night and I was really pretty drunk, I could hardly see straight. I had had a great time, or so I thought. A crowd of boys started following me, all laughing. At first it was just fun but then it got nasty. I ended up in the gutter and then in hospital that night. Really knocked about. They had raped me one after another. It might never have happened if I hadn't been drinking.'

When she recovered Lucy got a job as a fashion model. In three years she became very successful. She had cut back on her drinking for a while after the shock of her experience in the street, but she found it extremely hard. Her parents were thrilled with her success, her fame and seeing her pictures in glossy magazines, and they were inclined to pass off the odd occasion when she drank too much as youthful high spirits.

She began to have trouble with her weight, with the hours, with the parties and mostly with the drinking. It was all beginning to count. She got more anxious about assignments and the more anxious she became, the more she drank. After breaking a couple of important dates with photographers, her agency first warned her and then let her go. She couldn't stop.

'I knew I was on the slippery slope,' says Lucy, 'the drinking had taken over. I didn't think so at the time, it was everyone else's fault, the agency's, the photographers', my parents', even the weather if it suited me. At this point I really started to drink daily. I was in a mess. I didn't care how I looked, or what I did. I tried to keep busy, I tried to get jobs, I went to parties, I slept around and I hated myself.

'One day I threw up in a public toilet and that was the pits. I determined to stop. I did for three days; I have never felt so ill in all my life. I shook, I vomited, I sweated – and I drank to make those feelings go away. By then I had started to look awful. I couldn't hold down a job. I couldn't get up in the morning. My friends were all getting fed up with me.'

Lucy tried many jobs in the next few years, getting more sick, more desperate and more full of self-disgust. For a while she worked as a prostitute but ended up in hospital after a beating. In the next five years she was admitted nine times to psychiatric hospitals for her alcoholism. She abused tranquillisers for a while to try and get herself together, but before long she returned to her drug of choice: alcohol.

'I became bitter, angry, blaming the whole world and marinating in self-pity,' says Lucy. 'I thought of suicide but something stopped me. I never believed I was an alcoholic – after all, by now I was only twenty-eight and alcoholics . . . they're old people . . .' Lucy, amazingly, still presented quite an attractive appearance, but inside she felt dreadful.

In this state she came for treatment. Her GP, her parents and her friends had told her it was her last chance. They were sick of her promises, her anger and her blaming. The first few days she was quite subdued but then she started complaining, sulking, picking on the other patients and generally being a pain in the neck. When confronted with this she stormed out of the room. 'I am not going to be treated like a child. F— off,' she told the staff. When told that she could either settle down or leave she was so surprised that her mouth fell open. She had intimidated staff in hospitals for years, mostly to get a comfortable 'doss' for the winter.

Lucy was asked to write down examples of the way her drinking had hurt herself and others. For days she refused and played the victim. 'I have never hurt anybody. They all hurt me,' she insisted. Gradually she began to realise that if she looked at her drinking honestly she could see that, as it had progressed, her life had fallen apart. And it was *not* as she had always told herself, that 'I drink because life has been so rough on me.'

It took many weeks for Lucy to accept that it is all right to be a recovering alcoholic, that she is a worthwhile person and that there is hope. She became more attractive as the days passed, not just physically but as a human being.

She says, 'I feel clean for the first time since I was a kid. For years I have felt dirty and mucky inside. The more I drank to get away from that feeling, the worse it got. I had everything in life, a good home, super parents, love and affection, an education – and I blew it. Booze really lost me everything of value.'

Lucy left treatment happy, a bit fearful but determined to make it. She went to secretarial college and did very well. She found a job in a travel agency and loves it.

'I like myself at last. I can glance in the mirror and not want to throw up at the look in my eyes. I can go out on dates and enjoy myself without a drink. I've just had a promotion too. My parents don't look old and tired any more when they see me. There is a light back in their faces. I go to AA [Alcoholics Anonymous] regularly and meet up with other recovering people like me. It makes sense. I need that support to maintain a normal and happy life. We have a lot of good laughs and the people in AA are always there for me if I need them. I don't need a drink, I don't want a drink and I am not ashamed any more of being an alcoholic. I got sick, I got help and I am well. It's great.'

PART TWO

The Harm of Alcoholism

2

Alcoholism: Breaking
the Stereotypes

Alcoholism is tragically and fundamentally misunderstood. Every part of the disease is distorted by myth and coloured by opinions which have no firm basis in fact. If the alcoholic is ever to recover, the truth about alcoholism must be understood and the myths must be attacked and destroyed.

Myths surrounding alcoholism

'Isn't she disgusting?'
  'He is so pathetic.'
  'What an embarrassing evening it was; why can't he hold his drink like a man?'

Such comments show that many still think of alcoholism as a moral issue. Alcoholics are bad and nasty moral degenerates or worse – weak-willed and wet. 'They should just shape up!'

Most of us will happily laugh at the comic drunk on TV or feel infinitely superior as we wrinkle our nose as the skid-row bum makes his way past us on the street, leaving behind him a bouquet of stale wine, fumes and human grime.

But look in the mirror. If you like to 'get up' or 'out of it' with alcohol, there is a chance you may be an alcoholic.

What is alcoholism?

Alcoholism is a chronic illness resulting in an ever increasing dependence on alcohol, with an associated decline in physical and emotional health, an impairment of relationships at home and at work, and a deterioration in personal standards of behaviour.

Who is an alcoholic?

An alcoholic is a person with the illness of alcoholism regardless of whether he is initially a light, moderate or heavy drinker. Dependence is an illness of the body and the mind, but mostly an illness of the emotions.

The scale of the problem

It is accepted by licensed victuallers that there are at least **750,000** alcoholics in this country. The illness affects not only themselves, but also their families, friends, colleagues and places of work. *People in Britain drink nearly double what they drank in 1960* and women have nearly caught up with men with regard to the number of alcoholics, which is now approximately a 2:3 ratio. The illness is found in all areas of society. Industry, in particular, is suffering, from the company director to the tea lady.

In the United States, research has been going on for some years into the damage caused by alcoholism in all areas of society. Figures published in the late 1970s show that in the US $9.35 billion was lost in terms of production, $8.29 billion in medical services, $6.44 billion in traffic-accident costs, $0.51 billion in legal costs, $0.64 billion in treatment and rehabilitation programmes – making a total of $25.23 billion.

In Britain it has been shown recently that *alcoholism costs £1.5 billion a year*, with a loss to industry of some £600 million a year. There has been an enormous increase in hospital admissions, drink-driving offences, child battering, violence and accidents – all related to alcohol abuse.

As long as all sections of society, including management, unions, personnel, occupational health professionals and individuals continue to deny the problem of alcoholism and treat it as a moral issue rather than a treatable illness, this sad state of affairs will only worsen.

Alcohol is only addictive in a small percentage of the population. Why this is so remains a mystery, but it is a fact. Most people can drink in a social, non-harmful and enjoyable way. Others have an illness called alcoholism which progressively causes a great deal of harm. Alcoholics may be daily drinkers, evening drinkers, weekend drinkers or binge drinkers. They will become addicted no matter how much they drink.

Alcoholism is a sneaky illness; it slips up on a person in a subtle and insidious way. Many potential alcoholics talk about their drinking as fun, and early on it usually is. They enjoy themselves and many suffer rarely from hangovers. Some alcoholics have little trouble physically with alcohol. In fact they develop a high tolerance to it in their teens and twenties and are usually the ones who put everyone else to bed. As time goes on they often drink heavily on a fairly regular basis but can still work to a remarkably high standard.

Alcoholics are people like us

Some people find it incredible to think of responsible people like solicitors, doctors, nurses and even nuns as alcoholics. It offends their comfortable, detached idea that alcoholics are not people like us. That is why alcoholics suffer for so long. It is an illness, and is no more caused by background, education, profession, sex or religion than are diabetes or cancer. You would laugh if someone said, 'Smith cannot have cancer – he's a vicar,' but we find no problem with saying he couldn't be an alcoholic because he is a vicar.

For years people from every walk of life suffer emotionally and physically, because society as a whole, and many of the helping professions in particular, still insist on seeing the alcoholic as a loser, a failure and a bum. Of course there are alcoholics who sit on park benches, swigging cheap wine out of a bottle hidden in a paper bag. But most alcoholics have a job, indeed many are highly successful for years; they include bankers, policemen and soldiers. Most alcoholics have been married for at least seven years and have a minimum of two children. Alcoholics are also women from all walks of life.

You begin to see that this illness is no respecter of persons. It is wrong to say that it is caused by either deprivation or privilege. You can be a dustman or in Debrett and still be an alcoholic. Rich or poor, black or white, Catholic, Protestant, Muslim or Jew, you can suffer from this illness.

Teenage drinking

The majority of people reading this book have probably previously held an image of the alcoholic as middle-aged or older. But today even teenagers are getting addicted to alcohol – as young as fourteen or fifteen years old. Two girls we treated last year were fourteen and drinking up to a bottle of spirits a day, usually lifted from supermarkets.

There is a tremendous emphasis at the moment on the drug problem, but the problem of teenage alcoholism is infinitely larger. Teenage boys are inclined to drink and get drunk to be *macho* and grown up: an initiation rite to manhood. Girls begin drinking to get over shyness or to 'belong' to a group. A percentage of these children never find the right balance and become dependent on alcohol very young, just as others become dependent on hard drugs.

It is vital that young people are educated to understand the effects of alcohol; they must be taught that it is not a soft drug, harmless in comparison to hard drugs.

Emma: *the story of a teenage alcoholic*

Emma is an alcoholic – she started drinking at school 'for fun'. When at school she used to bribe one of the cleaners to get her a couple of bottles of wine a day. 'It was just a giggle,' she says. In the holidays she developed a taste for more alcohol than she was able to get at school. She started pinching it out of her parents' cabinet and topped up the whisky with water. They never knew. When invited to parties she always had a couple of drinks before she went 'to give me confidence', and when she got there she always thought other girls drank very slowly.

When she was kicked out of school for bringing in 'pot', her parents still did not suspect a problem and put it down to teenage rebellion. She went to a sixth-form course at the local technical college and spent a lot of her time in wine bars. Her parents never found out. At this stage she had developed a massive tolerance to alcohol and never appeared drunk to her friends or family.

Increasingly, however, Emma was getting into more and more trouble. She started to have 'blackouts' – she could not remember how she got home or where she had left her car. On more than one occasion she woke up in bed with a man and couldn't remember how she had got there. She started to feel fearful and guilty, and drank more to deal with those feelings. She left the sixth-form course with her A-levels but they were not very good ones – not good enough for the university place which she had always wanted. She couldn't see the connection between her loss of functioning and her increased drinking.

Emma was pretty and had no shortage of boy-friends. At twenty she fell in love. She had met David at a sales conference at the office where she now worked as a secretary. They had a lot in common, they liked the same music and films, and Emma felt happier than she had for years. She noticed that David didn't drink the way she did but it didn't bother her unduly until one day he remarked on the fact that she had drunk two-thirds of a bottle of wine at dinner. She defended herself and said she had had a rough day. For a couple of weeks she watched herself but she couldn't keep it up. She started to drink quite heavily before she went to meet David. At first he said nothing, but just gave her the occasional odd glance.

Just before Christmas, about nine months after she had started dating David, he was up for promotion and was invited to have dinner with his boss and the boss's wife. He asked Emma to join him. Emma was nervous about this. She had her hair done and spent ages on her face and nails. But she couldn't quell the butterflies in her stomach – the feeling of dread. 'I'll just have one drink,' she said. By the time David picked her up she had had four double whiskies. David was furious when he smelt the whisky on her breath and drove off to the dinner party in silence. Emma fumed. She was resentful and sorry for herself: 'He doesn't know how it feels.'

At the restaurant Emma accepted the offer of a drink before dinner, giving David a glance which said, 'I'll show you.' There was wine with the dinner, both white and red. Emma became increasingly more talkative and loud. She laughed inappropriately and told a slightly offensive story, which did not go down well. There was an awkward silence.

David made moves to leave as soon as he conveniently could. In the car he raged at her: 'You selfish, stupid bitch – you may have ruined my job! You're drunk, you're always drinking.' The rest of the journey passed in silence. He did not get out of the car at her flat, just opened the door. She tried to talk to him, but he drove off without responding.

Inside the flat Emma cried tears of humiliation and rage. She was shaking as she picked up the whisky bottle and by midnight had drunk herself into oblivion.

For a week David did not call, but at last he met her for dinner. He told her he could not go on. He cared about her but he couldn't stand her drinking and the constant fear of how she might behave. She was shattered. Back in her flat, she sat on her bed and cried her heart out. She was frightened and humiliated. She started to rage at David in her mind: 'I'll show the bastard.' She reached for the whisky and found the bottle almost empty. She remembered the late-night supermarket and quickly ran down the stairs and out into the street. She reached it just before it closed. By 2 a.m. she was very drunk, sobbing pathetically and deter-mined to get back at David. She lurched to the bathroom cupboard and took out the razor she used for shaving her legs. After a couple of half-hearted attempts at cutting her wrists she passed out on the bathroom floor.

Her landlady heard Emma's cat miaowing early next morning and let herself into the flat when Emma didn't answer the door. She found her still passed out on the bathroom floor, stinking of whisky, the blood dry on her wrists. She phoned her own sister who happened to be in AA, and got Emma into treatment.

Emma is an alcoholic who nearly died of this illness before her twenty-first birthday. Alcoholism induces self-pity and blaming of others. Emma denied her problems with drink instead of getting help for it. A teenager as a chronic alcoholic does not fit with the picture most of us have of alcoholism. Attempting suicide in alcoholic self-pity seems melodramatic, but it happens. Emma could have died. Hers was not a problem of a broken romance but the illness of alcoholism.

Think of alcoholism as a disease, not a disgrace – an illness, not an issue concerning morality or weakness. Then the sick person will get treatment rather than stigma and rejection. If you think of an alcoholic as someone permanently drunk or incoherent then you will not recognize your alcoholism or your alcoholic. It is like a man who went to the funeral of an acquaintance. He asked his wife of what illness the acquaintance had died. She said, 'He was an alcoholic.' 'Did he go to Alcoholics Anonymous?' said the man. 'Oh no,' said the wife, 'he wasn't that bad.' That man need not have died. One of the many myths surrounding alcoholism killed him.

Most people would accept that it makes sense to identify an illness early and treat it. Yet with alcoholism, our ignorance and misconceptions prevent this happening.

3

Damage to the Alcoholic

Very few people who drink have any idea of what alcohol actually does *to* them. They know what alcohol does *for* them – it alters the mood and gives a feeling of well-being. But most people are abysmally ignorant of what alcohol does to *harm* them.

The first stage in doing something about alcoholism is to learn a little about alcohol itself.

What is alcohol?

The majority of the population uses a drug which has a varied and sometimes harmful action. This is alcohol, or ethanol, a colourless inflammable liquid. It is known to have been the basis of intoxicating drinks since approximately 6000 BC. It is produced by the action of yeast fungi, which ferment certain sugars to exhaustion point. This process eventually produces alcohol. Alcoholic drinks are mainly ethyl alcohol and water, but they also contain other substances called congeners, which are used to give colour and flavour to individual drinks. These contribute to the causes of a hangover.

Alcohol is absorbed into the body via the stomach and the intestines. It is passed round the body by the bloodstream to all the major organs, especially the liver and brain. The rate of absorption can be influenced by certain circumstances such as food in the stomach (which slows down absorption) or carbonation in drinks such as sparkling wine or the soda in whisky and soda (which accelerates absorption and of course the speed of effect).

The size of the drinker is certainly a factor. Obviously if an eight-stone woman drinks the same quantity as a sixteen-stone man she is going to get drunker more quickly and probably in a more damaging way.

Alcohol is metabolised or burned off by the body. It can stay in the bloodstream for a long time; it does not matter if there are many hours between drinks. In fact if you have been drinking late at night and get up in the morning to go to work you could still be breathalysed as clinically drunk. Alcohol is removed from the blood at a rate of about 15mg/100ml per hour, so there is no way to hurry this process. Don't kid yourself that you can drink a pint of black coffee and be sober. All you would become is a very wide-awake drunk!

Is alcoholism hereditary?

There is evidence that alcoholism is hereditary. There have been studies done in Britain, Denmark and the US with identical twins, one of whom was raised with an alcoholic and one in a non-alcoholic family. It appears that there is just as high an occurrence of alcoholism with the twin raised in the non-drinking environment as with the one who was raised with the alcoholic. This indicates a genetic rather than an environmental factor. Also, sons of alcoholics who are adopted in early life are four times more likely to become alcoholic than adoptees without alcoholic biological parents. From observation over nearly twenty years of working with alcoholics, we find that at any given time over 50 per cent of the alcoholics in treatment will have at least one alcoholic parent or grandparent.

Alcoholism as a physiological illness

Because of the myths about alcohol, the drinker, his family, his doctor and his employer may innocently collude in the drinker's becoming progressively more dependent on alcohol. Many times we have seen men and women who have had an annual medical check-up and have been told, 'Your liver tests are up a bit. Cut back on the drinking for a couple of months.' If these people are alcoholic 'cutting back', even if they can manage it, will merely make them fit enough to drink again the way they want to.

Changing the flavour is another way that some drinkers tell themselves they are all right. 'I'll only drink beer or wine for a while; it's spirits that cause the problem.' This myth has killed a lot of people. And educated, intelligent and sometimes even medically trained people accept it as fact.

If you are drinking for the effect rather than the flavour all that happens is that you are going to drink the equivalent amount of wine or beer to give you the 'buzz' or lift you want. It is the alcohol content you are after and it is *that* which damages the body and the mind, regardless of flavour.

The early symptoms

Gradually, however, small incidents begin to occur that are warning signs. Upset stomachs, gastritis, a burning sensation which feels as if it is just below the breast bone. Sometimes diarrhoea of unknown origin. Not wanting to eat and ending up having only liquid lunches, i.e. booze. Skipping meals altogether as more time is spent in the pub or downing the bottle of wine at home alone or with a bunch of friends.

Damage to the digestive system

The whole of the digestive system can be affected by alcoholic drinking. There are some more serious conditions. Drinkers are more prone to stomach ulcers and to cancer of the throat and mouth, although the latter may also be related to the fact that most alcoholics are also heavy smokers. There is likewise a higher incidence of cancer of the oesophagus, the tube from mouth to stomach; cancer of the stomach can also occur.

Alcoholics also often suffer from vitamin deficiency – caused by poor diet or poor absorption of essential vitamins and minerals – which is directly related to excessive drinking. Even eating a perfectly balanced diet cannot compensate because drinking kills vitamins. Taking handfuls of vitamins in the belief that they will counter-balance the effects of drinking is merely to kid yourself, as they have little chance of being absorbed.

Damage to the liver

One of the most commonly known effects of drinking is damage to the liver. One immediately thinks of cirrhosis, but in fact only a small proportion of alcoholics have this very unpleasant condition. The most common damage is hepatitis, inflammation of the liver. Some may develop what is called 'fatty liver', which can lead to cirrhosis. This is when the liver cannot cope with the amount of alcohol it is being asked to process and lays down fatty areas in the hepatic tissue. At this stage, if the person stops drinking, the liver can recover but if the disorder progresses to cirrhosis it is extremely dangerous.

To most alcoholics warnings are a waste of time. The alcoholic thinks 'it will never happen to me' and goes on insulting this struggling organ. The liver begins to be damaged by the continuing abuse. Basically cirrhosis is scarring of the liver. As you know, scars do not go away – perhaps you have old scars on your knees from childhood escapades. If the liver is continually abused it lays down more and more scar tissue until there is not enough liver left to cope with life. It is a very unpleasant way to go!

Another serious condition which relates to both the liver and the gastric system is oesophageal varices. This means that in the walls of the tube from the mouth to the stomach, the oesophagus, the veins swell and their walls become thin, rather like the large varicose veins seen in fat ladies. This is caused by the back-up of blood in the area due to damage of the liver. It is often fatal, as it is very hard to stop the bleeding.

The denial system – that is, the reluctance of alcoholics to accept that they are alcoholics – is so great that even with this serious condition alcoholics will ignore their drinking problem and continue to drink. Paul was forty years old when he came into treatment. He was very bright, had a good job and was married with three young daughters. After a few days he arrogantly decided he did not need help and *knowing* that he had this condition he went out and continued to drink. Three days later he had a massive bleed and died.

Damage to the heart

You would not think that the heart could be affected by drinking, but it is. The condition called alcoholic cardiomyopathy occurs – this is simply damage to the muscles of the heart. The heart is a pump and if it gets damaged it doesn't do its job properly and beats irregularly and inadequately. This puts enormous strain on it, and that can be dangerous.

Damage to the blood cells

The actual composition of red blood cells is changed by alcoholic drinking and a condition occurs called macrocytosis; in this the effect of alcohol in the bone marrow means that the red cells enlarge and are less efficient. There is also damage to the white blood cells, which is very dangerous because they combat infection.

There is another part of the blood affected, the platelets which help to clot the blood. If you have an ulcer and your platelets don't work and your infection-resisters don't work, you are in a lot of trouble.

All these changes in the blood return to normal if the alcoholic stops drinking.

Nervous system

Alcohol is a depressant not a stimulant. It is often erroneously thought to be the latter because people often become overly talkative or aggressive when drinking. This is called 'disinhibition' as the control areas in the brain are impaired. The exact way alcohol works in the brain is not entirely understood but changes take place in the drinker in relation to the quantity drunk.

The first stage is to feel carefree and released from ordinary fears and worries. At the second stage, where the alcohol intake is only 30 mg per 100 ml of blood – less than half of the 80 mg per cent which counts as 'over the limit' – more brain functions are impaired and driving skills and judgement are also affected. The third stage of physical and emotional clumsiness occurs at 100 mg per cent and at 200 mg per cent there is obvious impairment to movement and behaviour. The fourth stage is gross intoxication, confusion, 'passing out' and progressive stupor at approximately 300 mg per cent. Death occurs somewhere between 500 and 800 mg per cent. *Alcohol is a drug which can kill.*

People are inclined to think that 'blackouts' relating to drinking mean that the person passes out. Blackouts occur in people who have been abusing alcohol heavily. The part of the brain which records memory shuts off and although you may be talking, functioning, travelling, conducting lessons, driving a car – you cannot remember all or parts of the events when you sober up. A minor example of this is not remembering how you got home after a party. But a more serious case concerned a woman we knew who closed a deal in London and woke up in a hotel room in another city with a man sleeping beside her – she could not remember how she got there, who he was or what had happened during the three days in between. Not long ago we worked with a family where the father killed the mother in a drunken state, woke up to find her body lying beside him next morning and could not remember what had happened.

The nervous system can also be severely damaged by a condition called alcoholic polyneuropathy – a grand name for a very unpleasant condition which has various degrees of severity. Basically it is damage to the nerve endings. In a mild form it shows as numbness or tingling feelings in the extremities, usually starting in the feet. It might be accompanied by muscle damage. When it gets really bad the legs become wasted, there is unsteadiness of gait and walking is difficult. Sensation in the legs is impaired. In severe cases the legs become useless. This can mend if the alcoholic stops drinking.

One of our patients arrived for treatment on crutches, a very frail man who had been an alcoholic for years, after serving as a regular soldier. He recovered and came to see us a year later and gave us his crutches as a souvenir.

DTs

DTs or delirium tremens is a condition which can occur when an alcoholic stops drinking abruptly.

At first the alcoholic is shaking, sweating, agitated, the pulse is rapid and the alcoholic is very fearful. If he is untreated at this stage, hallucinations can occur. Usually objects in the room are distorted, especially patterned wallpaper or curtains. People laugh about 'pink elephants' but actually to experience grotesque and terrifying visions, often of insects, snakes or animals of some kind, is not funny at all. It is frightening to observe the condition in a patient, and quite appalling to experience.

A further complication of DTs is seizures or fits. These look just like epileptic fits, and can be dangerous, particularly if they occur outside a hospital environment. Patients can hurt themselves severely or inhale their vomit. One man who worked in a steel works, in the room where they stacked cut-off ends of steel, had a seizure. He cut his face, arms and legs to ribbons on the edge of the steel. Another case concerned a woman who had a fit and fell into a fire, seriously burning herself all down her back, in some places right through to the bone. She spent months in hospital having skin grafts.

Korsakoff's psychosis

This is rare, but it does happen to alcoholics. It means that the person loses recent memory completely. In one large psychiatric hospital there was an elderly man looking at himself in a mirror and crying because he thought he should see himself as a young man. When his wife came to see him he would get very upset as he had no recollection of her growing old and only remembered her as young. It was heartbreaking to watch.

The emotional harm of alcohol

So far we have talked about the physical effects of drinking, but the emotional and psychological damage that increases over the years can be just as damaging for the drinker, and even more so for the people around in his or her life.

Many alcoholics have the same emotional problems as everyone else before they start drinking. These problems are aggravated, however, by their addiction to alcohol. Alcoholism undermines and lessens the alcoholic's ability to cope with the normal problems of living. Furthermore, the alcoholic's emotions become exaggerated as the illness progresses.

Some alcoholics are arrogant. They have a massive ego and a very low sense of self-worth. They are full of stubborn pride, yet at the same time full of self-hatred. This is not helpful if they are trying to learn anything, because they think they know it all.

Alcoholics tend to be over-sensitive. They cannot take criticism and therefore are unable to learn about themselves. They can be very defensive, exquisitely sensitive to self and totally insensitive to the feelings of others. A boy we had in treatment was upset because he had not had any visitors the week before. His sister called, crying because she had been sexually molested in a park while out walking her dog. He said, 'Yes, but why didn't you visit me last week?' She was shattered by his response. This self-obsession is part of the illness.

Alcoholics wallow in self-pity. Oh, how they feel sorry for themselves. 'It's not fair – why me?' is the eternal cry. Alcoholics don't recognise this as self-pity. They usually call it depression – it's nicer and sounds better!

A good number of alcoholics get diagnosed as depressive when they really are not. Alcohol is a depressive drug – if you drank heavily you'd be depressed! It's a nice excuse to go on drinking, though. Some alcoholics get so low they think about overdoses and suicides. It's usually attention-getting and manipulative. 'You'll be sorry when I'm gone' is the feeling. It is angry and vindictive, and it sometimes backfires when the alcoholics are so drunk that they succeed. Most of the alcoholics we have known over the years who attempted suicide either did it to punish some family member who had confronted their drinking, or did it simply out of maudlin self-pity and guilt. When sober they freely admit, 'I wouldn't have had the guts.'

Alcoholics cannot bear frustration. They don't like being thwarted and behave like a baby in its cot who howls with rage when the teat of the bottle falls out of its mouth. There is a compulsive need for instant gratification – I want it *now*.

Alcoholics can also be angry and resentful people. There is often an inner, simmering, festering anger – sometimes smiling anger.

Alcoholics are sometimes great blamers and if it's someone else's fault it follows they don't have to change themselves.

Alcoholics do not want to accept reality. They are not good at accepting the ordinary discomforts of life. They feel it should not happen to them. They cannot face unpleasant facts and events and prefer to find oblivion, however terrifying. They put off unpleasant tasks and so make the situation worse.

Alcoholics are frightened. They may appear all tough and together but underneath there is tremendous fear – a deep inexplicable fear which becomes terror at the thought of stopping drinking. Some become paranoid and are so fearful of people that the distrust and suspicion become crippling. Often they use anger as a cover for fear – fear of opening bills, of answering the telephone, of meeting people; fear of rejection, fear of failure, even fear of trying in case they are not perfect.

Alcoholics are dishonest. They lie about their drinking to themselves and to their family and friends. They lie in order to go on drinking. This dishonesty becomes second nature and they lie even when they don't have to. They even have difficulty being honest with themselves.

All this can change if the alcoholic stops drinking and works on recovery.

5

Damage to Family and Friends

The isolation and frustration of the alcoholic family

The cry of the husband or wife of the alcoholic is often 'They get all the attention while drinking, all the attention during treatment and all the attention in recovery. What about *my* feelings?'

The pain and anger in this statement indicate the isolation and frustration of the family of the alcoholic. You only have to open a newspaper to read of incidents of violence, sometimes even murder, resulting from alcoholic behaviour in a family. Sometimes it is the family that gets beaten up, but sometimes the family are driven to violence themselves. In either case the emotional damage is profound and the effects of it last for years.

In one family two terribly frightened and bewildered children were sent into care and referred for counselling when their father, having drunk more than usual, picked a fight with the mother and strangled her. He woke in the morning to find her dead in bed. He had no recollection of what had happened, he had always loved her and his grief and remorse were terrible to see.

An eighteen-year-old, Irene, was sent to gaol for the killing of her father. For years he had made their home life a hell, he had repeatedly taunted and humiliated his wife and had accused his two teenage daughters of being 'whores'. They were in fact just schoolgirls. One night, Irene couldn't stand his verbal and physical abuse of her mother any more, and she went for him with a kitchen knife. In the struggle the knife went into his abdomen and cut a main artery. He bled to death before he arrived at the hospital. The family are still paying the price.

These are dramatic incidents, but *nearly a million families* in this country today are under the kind of emotional strain that ultimately makes many family members feel murderous, even if they don't act on it. Time and again we hear frightened and angry children cry, 'I wish he was dead!' Before families get to this state there are often years of anxiety, moments of hope and then despair again.

Living with the illness of alcoholism is increasingly more painful

Early in any relationship with an alcoholic there is little sign of a problem. Usually husband and wife go out together to the pub, a dance or a dinner party. Slowly and insidiously the wife may notice that her husband seems to drink more than anyone else. She doesn't take much notice.

But then at weekends he seems to get home later and later from the pub at lunch time. And during the week, before coming home from work in the evening, he again stops off at the pub. He begins to give excuses such as 'Oh, I was late at the office,' or 'I had to go and see so and so on the way home.' With a little checking she usually finds out that this is a lie.

She begins to get a bit irritated at the spoilt meals and she feels taken for granted. When she tells him, he gets defensive and may even start to blame her nagging for his staying out! So what does she do? She shuts up. She begins to question herself and says, 'Maybe I am being unreasonable.'

Over the years these small incidents add up. He starts to drink more when they are out with friends and gets silly or embarrassing. Sometimes he gets very personal about his wife or starts pawing other women. Maybe he just gets loud and she feels very embarrassed for him. After the children start to arrive she thinks he will settle down, and maybe for a time he does; but before long he is back into the same pattern of drinking.

Nell and Bill

Nell was very hurt when her husband Bill didn't even come to the hospital the day their first child was born. He was too busy out getting drunk with his mates, 'celebrating', as he put it. When she told him how hurt she was, he just couldn't see why she should be upset. The drinking was already making him totally insensitive to anybody's needs but his own.

Over the years a wife tries everything to help or change the alcoholic, desperately trying to hold on to the image of that person whom she loved but who is fast disappearing. The hurts, the slights, the put-downs, the emotional humiliation of living with a drinking alcoholic are enormous. It may not so much be the dramatic violence as the constantly renewed hope and then despair that destroy a relationship.

Jill and Andrew

Jill has never been abused physically but when her husband Andrew drinks, nothing is ever right. 'Jill, you know I dislike that dress, why do you wear it?' 'Jill, you really shouldn't have spoken as you did at dinner, you don't really know what you are talking about.' In fact he had been the one who had gone on and on and had topped every story with another, boring the dinner guests with his know-it-all remarks, until there was an awkward silence.

This leaves Jill always feeling wrong. Whatever she says she is made to feel stupid or pointless. She feels undervalued and boring. Gradually and inevitably her already low self-esteem reaches the point where she now feels totally inhibited and immobilised and therefore unable to change her situation.

As Andrew's behaviour deteriorates, Jill becomes more and more isolated. She is embarrassed to tell her parents what is going on because after all they had raised doubts about him when she got married. She doesn't tell her friends because she feels it is disloyal and letting her husband down. She starts to tell lies, which makes her feel even more 'bad'. She covers up for him, excuses him, pretends everything is okay. When he starts being too hung over to get to work on Mondays, she is the one who calls up the office and lies for him.

The more Jill desperately tries to maintain normality the more he abuses and blames her. She tries being nice, she tries being a bitch, she uses sex and then withdraws it. She tries having a new hairdo. She tries spending more time with him than with the children and whatever she does and to whatever lengths she goes, in the end he always makes her feel that somehow she is to blame.

She starts fighting back but this doesn't work either. The evenings become cat-and-dog fights and he rushes out to the pub yet again.

She feels helpless, hopeless and abandoned. She has no career, she married early, she has no training, and she has little money of her own. Even if she wanted to leave she knows she can't as she feels she has no resources with which to survive in the world with herself and her children. Jill is trapped and afraid. She has kept most of this to herself. It's not surprising that she has become emotionally crippled.

Men suffer just as much if the woman is the drinker. It is easy to say it is better for a man: sometimes men have the advantages of greater financial security and a career. But they suffer just as much emotionally.

The self-obsession and insensitivity of alcoholics

One of the most painful aspects for people living with an alcoholic is the progressive insensitivity.

It has been said that the most important part of the word alcoholism is 'ISM' – I, SELF and ME. Alcoholics over the years become exquisitely sensitive to self and almost totally insensitive to the feelings of others. They become the centre of their own universe. Many times we have heard men and women say, 'Well, they don't care about me, they won't stick with me. No wonder I drink.'

It never seems to occur to the alcoholic that it is because he or she is smelly, drunk and insensitive, and only looking out for his or her own satisfaction, that a wife or husband feels anything from distaste to downright revulsion at times. But when this is expressed, it is just another 'reason' for the alcoholic to drink on.

Family guilt

Many times wives and husbands are also damaged by accepting advice from the ignorant. Unless you work directly with alcoholics for a long time, their stories and reasons and excuses for drinking are totally believable.

Many friends, families, doctors and social workers fall for the notion that the stress makes the drinker. In fact the drinkers create their own stress by their lack of performance and their diminished functioning as the drinking progresses. All these well-meaning people are inclined to say such things as 'Try being nicer to him, take her out more, it must be because you spend too much time at your work.' The spouses are then made to feel more guilty and responsible, and they begin to believe that perhaps it really is their fault. You can imagine what this will do to an already shattered self-worth. It never seems to occur to people to say, 'It must be awful being nice to that chap who is such a pain in the neck all the time,' or 'I wonder if that chap stays out late because she is not much fun to come home to. She looks such a mess, she's a real bitch when she drinks.'

The alcoholic has a marvellous capacity to present himself as a victim, of the family, the boss, the job and even the whole world. In fact the alcoholic, although suffering a great deal, is most of the time anaesthetised to emotional pain. It is the family that is the victim. The wife or the husband on the receiving end often becomes quite emotionally damaged by living in a constant state of anxiety and fear.

Maggie had to be medically treated for anxiety after ten years of never knowing how or when her husband would turn up. He was a gentle, loving person when they first met, and she had never seen the other side of him. Early on in the marriage he started to drink more and more. There was nothing wrong at work, there was nothing wrong with their relationship, he just liked to drink and he drank more and more regularly. After four or five years she knew that he would be in late from work, there were always excuses, there were always reasons. Sometimes he would just be half an hour late, sometimes he wasn't in until 11.00 p.m. But if she didn't have supper ready, if he was early, then she was to blame. If it was all curled up and dried when he came in late, then that was wrong too.

After a while he started going on to drinking clubs and sometimes he wouldn't come home until two or three in the morning. He would either be 'up' and full of himself and wanting sex, or he would be morose and bad-tempered and looking for an argument. Sometimes he wouldn't arrive home at all and she lived with the fear of a phone call from the police or a hospital. All the time he looked quite good physically, held down a good job and to most of the world he was a hell of a guy. But Maggie knew the real person she was living with, and the fear became too much to bear.

Looking after yourself

It is vital that you – the wife, the husband or family member – should take care of yourself. It doesn't matter whether the alcoholic has gone into treatment, is recovering in AA, is perhaps still drinking, or even dies of the illness; it is essential that you too should take care of yourself and your emotions.

You have rights too, you are a person, you are worthwhile, you need to be happy and balanced and able to cope with normal life. You have a right to some peace, love, a caring family and a career. So start today taking care of yourself.

Emotional harm is just as damaging as physical harm. Whether you are hurt emotionally or battered physically, you don't have to accept it. Battered wives are often found in alcoholic marriages. You have been made to feel so worthless so many times that you seem to accept the beatings as normal. The abnormal has become normal for you through habit. The fear of getting out, of being on your own, is greater than putting up with the misery, for yourself and your children.

You don't have to feel helpless, you can get help, if you are willing.

It is only when you start looking after yourself that you realise that **you won't get anywhere unless the alcoholic accepts the need for recovery**. A husband cannot treat his alcoholic wife any more than he could if she had cancer. A wife cannot cure her alcoholic husband any more than she could if he had heart disease.

If you try to control and fix the situation yourself, you will only end up experiencing the most appalling fear, loneliness, pain and suffering.

Both the alcoholic *and* his family need help and, as we will see in Parts Three and Four, the best places to get it are Alcoholics Anonymous and Al-anon, the family part of AA.

5

Damage to the Children of Alcoholics

Emotional abuse

Countless times we have heard children of alcoholics talk of their fear, sometimes bordering on terror, mixed with hatred, guilt and loneliness.

A little boy of four was so frightened of what would happen when his father came home from the office and found the mother drinking that he would literally drag her to bed and pretend to himself that she had a cold; he would repeat this to his father and then be told not to lie. She used to be sick quite often, and he used to clean it up, to hide it from the father so there wouldn't be a row when he came in.

Don't ever tell yourself that children are too young to understand.

One two-and-a-half-year-old told his mother, 'Mummy, I don't like coming near you when you drink, you smell bad.' This was after she had been sober for two weeks, and she was shocked and horrified because she had no idea that he knew. He also told her a little while later that he was glad that she was not drinking that 'loony juice' anymore which made her act 'mad'. And these two statements from a small child provided the turning point in her recovery, when she really recognised the damage that she had been causing to her child.

Families can be wrecked by alcoholism, and children become totally immobilised, frightened and panic-stricken by what is going on.

Many children of alcoholics feel somehow that they are at fault: 'If she loved me she wouldn't drink, so she doesn't love me.' They then inevitably jump to the heart-rending conclusion: 'so there is something wrong with me.'

Living in a house with an alcoholic mother or father is profoundly destructive to the entire family. There are other equally stressful situations. Children of alcoholics do not have the sole rights to pain but not many illnesses are so permanent or so damaging in their long-term effect.

If you have children or if you are the child of an alcoholic, you can do something about your own feelings and emotions. You don't have to go on being a victim, you don't even have to stay with the situation.

The repression of emotion

Some children react to the disease in the home by being 'super good'. Other mothers will often say 'Oh, if only I had a child who was that polite and worked so hard at school.' This child is the coper, the fixer – the child that helps out at home, gets good marks at school, takes care of the other children and doesn't have tantrums. This child blocks up all his or her feelings. This child has learned it doesn't pay to show emotion. One minute he or she gets love and affection from the drinking father and the next abuse. There is absolutely no connection between what he or she does and how the father reacts, so this child thinks, 'If I am good and clever then maybe there will be less trouble.' Some turn all their feelings inwards and so never learn how to express themselves. This is crippling in later life.

One small boy of thirteen, *Tony*, was frightening in his maturity. His father was alcoholic and his mother was pregnant with her fourth child. 'I had to look after things at home,' he said calmly. 'Dad was drunk most of the time. He went to work but you never knew how he would be when he came home. Mum was very upset all the time and couldn't cope with the other kids, so I did.'

Tony confided no feeling, no emotions for several sessions. It came out that he cooked most of the meals, took the children to school, even handled most of the housekeeping money. His mother had become too anxious to cope with these domestic chores and her alcoholic husband. She became completely indecisive, and Tony in fact made all the important decisions in the house.

On about the fourth or fifth session Tony at last broke down. His icy calm and his desperate loyalty to his parents deserted him. 'I hate him, I hate him,' he sobbed. 'Why won't he just go away? I wish he were dead.' In an instant this frighteningly adult child had become a heartbroken, weeping little boy.

The lack of security and stability

Children of alcoholics never have any security and stability in their lives.

Dad promises to mend the bike on Saturday, but when Saturday comes he is either hung over from Friday night or is having a lie-in and gets up late just in time to go to the pub again. He spends his afternoon watching sport on the television drinking canned beer, and then is off out again. The child hopes that this weekend it will be different and says, 'Dad, you promised.' Dad reacts to this with a clip round the ear or it ends up in a shouting match, and soon the child stops asking.

Julia was fourteen, her mother had been drinking as long as she could remember. She dreaded coming home from school – what would she find? She knew her mother would be drunk, but how drunk?

Sometimes when she was younger her mother would meet her from school in the car. 'I used to hate her coming. All the other Mums would be chatting and nice. Mum would drive up and she would look awful. She had been drinking and she was a bit wobbly. She would look silly. I used to be embarrassed. I hated getting into the car and was so scared as she used to drive very fast and would hit the kerb stones as we went round the corners. I had a big lump in my stomach all the time and thought she would crash any minute.

'She was too tired, as she put it, to cook the tea for Dad and my brother, so I did it. She would lie on the sofa with another drink and Dad would come in and his face looked so sad. If he said anything she would start being horrid to him and shouting at him that he was no good and a lousy husband. On and on and on until he lost his temper and shouted at her and sometimes he would hit her he was so angry. I used to hide in my bedroom and put the pillows over my head, and inside I was screaming too.'

Some children of alcoholics act out their own fear and anger in a destructive way.

Tim started playing truant when he was about ten. He was a nice little kid but he couldn't stand what was going on at home. He started fooling around in class and never did his homework. At home he would sulk and have a tantrum, and at twelve he was sent home from school for smoking.

Mum was at her wits' end with Dad's drinking and taking care of the other children. Tim was too much and she couldn't cope with him. He started to stay out all hours and was picked up for shoplifting at fourteen. She was too ashamed to tell the social worker about the drinking husband.

At fifteen Tim started smoking pot and by the time he was sixteen and a half he was drinking heavily, usually stealing the money from his mother or shoplifting for the money. By eighteen he had been arrested three times for being drunk. By nineteen he was using speed as well as the pot and had started using heroin regularly. He rarely went home except for a change of clothes.

His father started to realise even through his drinking that there was something wrong with his son; he tried to tell Tim to get off the drugs and suggested that he was a loser. Tim just looked at him and then screamed at him, 'Who the hell are you to talk? Screw you, you miserable old drunk.' Shortly afterwards Tim was arrested for possession of drugs and sent to prison.

Associated dependencies

Children of alcoholics find it almost impossible to talk about their feelings. They never learn to trust anyone; since they see so much dishonesty, why should they? They spend all their young lives holding down their feelings. They never have any practice sharing them, so how on earth can they identify what they really do feel?

Some children, like Tim, become dependent themselves. It is sometimes alcohol but it can be drugs.

A significant number of children, usually girls, who are children of alcoholic fathers develop anorexia or bulemia. Girls with either of these problems describe a terrible sense of worthlessness when they eventually open up and start to trust others. They have no self-worth. They have spent their young lives trying to be perfect. They are usually very bright and totally unable to talk about feelings. They become convinced that the only desirable body image is a thin one, and their pursuit of this objective goes out of control just like any other addiction.

There is an enormous reservoir of anger towards the alcoholic parent, usually unexpressed and totally self-destructive. Even when the alcoholic parent recovers, the child is left with a legacy of crippling emotions.

One child, *Peg*, took weeks and weeks even to talk of her fear and anger about her father's drinking and the appalling incidence of emotional battering that had gone on for years. She didn't tell him then as that would have been pointless. She was scared to tell him now because he was in recovery and she felt that it might make him drink again, not understanding that the alcoholism was *his* problem. At some level Peg felt that it was all her responsibility, her fault. She took all the trauma in the family on her shoulders. Not eating was the one thing she felt she could control in the chaos around her. Then this too went out of control, doubling her feelings of panic, confusion and worthlessness.

When an alcoholic's children grow up into adults, they have usually never talked about their feelings and the emotional and physical damage they have experienced. They have never learned to trust, they have never learned to feel properly, they have never learned to share – they can be very damaged people.

Time and again we have seen young adults stagger from one lousy relationship to another. If it is a daughter of a drinking father then her role model of a man is a very disturbed one. A high proportion of daughters of alcoholic fathers marry alcoholics unknowingly. It is a personality type with which she is familiar and feels comfortable.

A son of an alcoholic has very ambivalent feelings about women – 'I should love my mother', but he doesn't.

Learning to manipulate

Another result of being the child of an alcoholic is learning to manipulate. For years they see the alcoholic manipulating everybody with charm, with promises seldom kept and with lies. They learn manipulation from the cradle. It is not long before they know *when* to ask Dad or Mum for money – usually it is when they are in a stage of mellowness or full of remorse after a drinking bout. They have learned to play one parent off against another. 'Mummy said I can.' Quite frequently the child will resent the non-drinking parent more than the drinker as the sober parent is desperately trying to hold on to some semblance of order to demonstrate love and discipline which is constantly sabotaged by the alcoholic.

Physical abuse

So far we have talked of harm to children in emotional terms. There are many cases where the violence becomes physical and children are hit or even regularly beaten in drunken fights. Sometimes the spouse colludes in covering this up. She is too ashamed to go to the social worker or the police. And she is frightened of even more violence from her husband. This cover-up behaviour just reconfirms her own sense of shame and worthlessness.

Most children we have known have had a safe place in the house – the bedroom, the loo, under the stairs, or down in the garden shed. They sit and escape into their own little fantasy worlds which make life bearable when reality becomes too hard to bear.

Sexual abuse, usually incest, is not unknown in alcoholic families. The fear and terror of small children, usually girls, is quite appalling. Some children never speak of it to their mother as somehow they believe that it is their fault. Some fathers indulge in this destructive behaviour on a long-term basis. The child is made to collude in it because the alcoholic manages to persuade the child that they are 'special friends'. Some mothers blind themselves to what is going on.

Male alcoholics can have sexual experiences while drinking that appal them when sober. One father sat weeping his heart out when his wife told him what he had done. He had little recollection of it as he was so drunk and promised it wouldn't happen again. He continued to drink and it did happen again, and a whole family was shattered.

Solutions

It is not enough to relate stories of damage to children – there have to be solutions. The most important thing for the family is to get help for *themselves*, not just to concentrate on getting help for the alcoholic. The best place for families to go to is Al-anon. There is also Alateen for the children. What a relief it is for wives, husbands and children to talk to other families who understand their problems without having to explain them. Many professionals working in this field subtly, or not so subtly, blame the family and don't realise that if they are emotionally sick it is usually the *result* of living with an alcoholic and it is *not* the cause of that alcoholic's drinking. No one can make an alcoholic drink.

As the last resort if the alcoholic won't stop drinking, get out. You don't have to go down the tube just because the alcoholic does.

Checklist for helping yourself and your children

1. *Stop denying the problem.* Face up to alcoholism in the family and get positive help.

2. *Educate yourself and the children about this disease.* Ignore the myths and discover the truth by joining Al-anon, talking to recovering alcoholics and reading the list of books in Appendix 4.

3. *Encourage the children to go to Alateen,* and if there is not an Alateen meeting in your area, get them to talk to children of your friends in Al-anon.

4. *Stop identifying with the alcoholic.* If he is miserable or low you don't have to take his feelings on yourself and your children. After all, it is *his* illness.

5. *Listen to the children.* You have probably been so busy trying to repair the alcoholic that you are not hearing the children, whether it is about the drinking problem or just about school and their growing pains.

6. *Stop hiding what is going on.* Children are much smarter than you think. If you are trying to intervene in the illness, for instance by letting him stay in his chair when he has passed out, or by not clearing up his sick and letting him see it next morning, tell the children why. Explain that he is a sick person not a bad person. That he loves them and that there is a way for him to recover, but first he has to feel the effects of his illness to recognise how sick he has become.

7. *Don't be scared to be loving and affectionate.* Hug them. You may have been so busy coping that you have forgotten to do these simple things. Children need the reassurance of physical contact and closeness. It is probably their only safe harbour in a frightening world.

8. *Don't be afraid to set limits on their behaviour.* Children must understand that you love them but that you don't always love their behaviour. They will not respect you or like you if you give in to them and make excuses for irresponsible behaviour because of the chaos at home. In the long run this will not help them to be stable adults.

9. *Let them take responsibility for their actions and their own mistakes.*

For instance, if they run out of pocket money don't let them manipulate you into giving more. How will they ever grow up and understand that they have to be responsible if you keep being responsible for them?

10. *Most of all, let the children know quite simply and clearly that the illness of alcoholism is treatable*. People do recover. Make it clear that it is not their fault or their responsibility to repair their alcoholic. Tell them they could be little angels or absolute devils and it will not change the drinker. Like most children they are probably a mixture. *Get some trust and open talking going in your home. This is the best way for you all to be emotionally more healthy.*

PART THREE

For Family and Friends

6

How Family and Friends Can Intervene

Alcoholism is a treatable illness

If you think there is somebody in your family with a drinking problem, you probably feel very anxious about it or very helpless – it's quite terrifying when you begin to see that someone you love, a husband, a wife or a child, is drinking too much and causing harm to themselves or others. A lot of the fear comes from ignorance about this illness – and alcoholism is an illness, which can be and is treated successfully.

Don't get into a panic or feel hopeless. Put all the old myths out of your head about drinkers and drinking. A lot of people continue to believe that their loved ones don't have a drinking problem until they are reaching for the bottle in the morning. When you live with it you begin to notice things far ahead of that. Alcoholism is an illness like any other; it can be treated by people who understand it. Alcoholics do get well and go on to lead happy and normal lives.

Families can indirectly help the alcoholic to recover. The way the family deals with the ill person in their family can increase their chances of recovery. Your actions and behaviour will make an enormous difference, if you make the effort to understand what these actions should be.

Tell-tale signs of alcoholism

One of the major problems facing the family of an alcoholic is their own unwillingness to accept that there is a problem or perhaps, their reluctance to believe the worst (as they see it). Nobody wants to admit that their husband or wife or child or parent may have a problem with alcohol, therefore they may try to avoid facing the truth.

Here are some of the indications by which a family can tell what is really going on.

Behaviour

Alcoholics usually start drinking in their teens, just like everyone else, but they begin, after a few years, to show inappropriate behaviour and mood swings and to be very self-centred. They may be inappropriately high on alcohol or utterly depressed for no good reason. Excuses start to flow about why they are late home or why they smell of alcohol. They start picking arguments and fights to justify themselves.

Appearance

Alcoholics in the early stages may show little physical evidence of drinking. In the late stages they are often flushed or sweaty. You can smell drink on their breath or you can smell alcohol on their clothes or their skin.

Sense of time

Alcoholics begin to lose their sense of time. They would prefer to go out at night and come home late, and they have difficulty getting up in the morning. Progressively there are problems getting to work or they ask you to make excuses for not going to work, and ask you to call the boss. You may also begin to notice that when they have been drinking, the next day they have difficulty remembering exactly what happened and may subtly or not so subtly check with you about their own behaviour. If their behaviour has been destructive and you tell them about it, they will often deny it completely or blame you, and usually this is because they can't really remember themselves how they behaved and so become very defensive.

Hiding drink

As the illness progresses you may notice alcohol in inappropriate places in the house. Sometimes it is hidden in very odd places: in the laundry basket, under the mattress, in the airing cupboard. Particularly with women, the hiding of alcohol becomes apparent as the illness progresses.

Apathy

As the progression of the disease advances, alcoholics begin to lose interest in outside things; activities and hobbies they once enjoyed drop away. It also seems to appear that old friends don't come around any more or you are not asked around to friends' houses. It seems that your only friends are people who drink as much as, if not more than, the drinking member of the family.

Alcoholics sometimes withdraw from family life. They are so busy going to the pub or maintaining their alcohol supply or coming in late from work that family life starts to disintegrate and they often do not turn up at home until the children are safely in bed, and then they often complain that the children aren't there to see them.

Ethical deterioration

Alcoholics show a kind of mental obsession with drink and drinking occasions and start to complain about work, colleagues and family. As dependence on alcohol gets worse the alcoholic becomes secretive, small lies become apparent, behaviour starts to be out of character. Even in front of the family's eyes they can change from being the caring, loving person they once were to a very unpleasant personality.

Illusion of well-being

It is important to realise that alcoholics differ. Some show the signs very quickly indeed and cannot conceal the problem from their family. In others alcoholism progresses very slowly and it may be quite a long time before the family realises what is going on. Some alcoholics manage to function quite well despite their illness. Company directors and television stars can be alcoholic, doctors and nurses, policemen and plumbers as well as meths drinkers in the gutter. Some alcoholics hold down good jobs for many years and have all the trappings of success, yet they may be dependent on drink.

How the family reacts

The family reacts to the drinking problem with fear, with hopelessness, with a sense that somehow they are responsible for the problem and with anger at the realisation of their own helplessness, as they see it. This is a very painful situation and the pain is sometimes almost indescribable. It is usually followed by a sense of rage and fury or sad resignation.

Family members start to ask themselves, 'What did I do wrong to cause this?' and they are often afraid or ashamed to let anybody outside the family know about it. The alcoholic will prey on this guilt.

Then a kind of emotional blackmail starts to show itself. The husband says, 'If you were different, if you were prettier, if you were sexier, if you were more intelligent, if you helped me more, then I wouldn't drink,' and the unfortunate wife begins to think this is true.

Or if it is a woman who is drinking she will hurl the same kind of abuse at her family and somehow manage to make her husband feel useless or inadequate and convince him that he is to blame.

Feeling isolated

Wives often tell us that their lives become more and more isolated because it's too embarrassing to ask friends home. The wife never knows how her husband is going to behave – he may be charm and grace personified over a meal with friends but he may become progressively more embarrassing, more maudlin, more aggressive, more humiliating, in his behaviour so that the fear of entertaining becomes greater than risking it.

So the wife becomes more and more isolated, more and more ashamed and feels she cannot talk to anybody. The wife is blamed in such a way that she is made to think of herself as a hindrance to her husband and his career, and the more she believes this the more immobilised she becomes.

'Repairing' the alcoholic

At this stage family members usually start a desperate search for a way to 'repair' their alcoholic. They go to doctors, family friends, clinics, anybody they may know who has had some experience, and everywhere they go they get different advice, and often feel increasingly hopeless.

Harry's story

Sometimes family members try and fix the problem themselves. Harry, for example, spent fifteen years trying to cure his wife in every way he could. Never in his life had he exerted such will power as in this battle, no other problem in his very successful career had ever required a fraction of the energy that he put into his unsuccessful attempt to solve this one.

'I was 47 years old when I hit bottom. In addition to being a husband and a father I tried to play the role of psychiatrist and priest. Only afterwards did I realise how crazy I was thinking I could play all the roles at the same time.

'The biggest mistake I made was that I tried to change another person, the one closest to me. I forgot how difficult it is to change myself even when it would be in my own best interest.

'What I learned is that I must first come to terms with myself. Without a calm and informed approach I couldn't do anything about this.

'I tried to cover up the alcohol problem my wife had for many years. She was already drinking out of control before I met her but I didn't realise it at the time. She seemed to be the life of every party. However, she just didn't seem to realise when the party was over. After some time I became embarrassed with her behaviour, cut down on the number of invitations we accepted, started to lie to friends that she was sick, took over responsibilities from her and made excuses. I pleaded with her, warned her and made threats that I did not carry out, because I always wanted to believe the promises she made.

'She then started to make excuses when I would no longer accept the promises. I was travelling too much or I was home too much, the children were too much for her to handle. A baby, another baby would solve the problem; a house full of animals would be the answer. We lived in a too isolated place, the city on the other hand is too noisy. It's too cold today, or too grey or too hot, and so on, and so on . . .

'I tried for years to follow her wishes, often not realising that they were contradictions of what she had said the day before. Fulfil her immediate desires then everything would be okay.

'Today it's clear how crazy this thinking was but as time passed I found it more and more difficult to live with her, myself and the children, and a hell on earth enveloped us all. We lived more and more with unresolved problems of the past, the anger and frustration of the day and the fear of what was going to happen tomorrow. To enjoy the day in which we were living was no longer possible. We were no longer able to help ourselves, only we couldn't see it.

'*At this point alcohol had taken control of our lives.* My wife actually was the first to realise this. Only then did we have a chance to win by giving up our fight to control this giant of alcoholism. To lose the battle, bury some of our pride, and ask for help.'

In this instance, both Harry and his wife Mary came for help.

You cannot control an alcoholic

Many families try for years to persuade their alcoholic to get help, and the alcoholic's response is usually, 'There is nothing wrong with me – if you changed, if life changed, if my boss changed, if the world changed, then I wouldn't drink.' Then the alcoholic goes off and deals with these problems with another drink.

Here are some of the things that people do to try and control the problem in vain attempts to stop the alcoholic drinking:

1. They ask the alcoholic to promise not to drink again. The alcoholic promises and then goes out for another drink.

2. They throw away the bottles, they hide them, they try to control the money. But the alcoholic just goes out and gets another drink.

3. They may weep, they may threaten, they may coax, they may bribe, they may nag. The alcoholic continues to drink.

4. They go to the family doctor, or the minister, or a friend, or a social worker to ask them to have a serious chat with the alcoholic. The alcoholic goes on drinking.

There are thousands more schemes and dodges and ideas and devices which the family tries in growing desperation. Some of them may result in the alcoholics stopping drinking for a few days or a few weeks, only to tell you they cannot be an alcoholic because they can stop, which of course is a myth. Any alcoholic can stop; it's learning how not to start again that is the problem.

But all of these devices miss the point:

Alcoholics will only stop drinking when they want to or when somebody else makes their drinking so uncomfortable that they have to ask for help.

What makes an alcoholic decide to stop?

Let's ask ourselves why alcoholics stop using alcohol and get well. Such a decision isn't easy. Alcoholics fear life without a drink almost as much as they fear going on drinking.

They stop only when in their own minds going on drinking seems even more painful than stopping.

Putting it another way, it's really when the consequences of drinking become too profoundly painful that an alcoholic will consider giving up the alcohol.

Sometimes it's the realisation that nobody is going to rescue them, bail them out, cover for them or lie for them any more. Families can raise this level of pain when they withdraw support and stop picking up the pieces. One woman who stopped drinking says, 'I only went for help and stopped drinking when my husband told me, "I love you but I cannot be around you," and pulled out of the family home. I was absolutely astounded and appalled. How on earth could this happen? And after three weeks I went to a treatment centre and joined Alcoholics Anonymous on leaving treatment.'

So the message is clear – **alcoholics stop drinking when the painful consequences of their drinking get too much to bear.** Family and friends must let the alcoholic experience those consequences. Stop smoothing the way for the alcoholic – it just enables the illness to continue.

Stop helping the alcoholic to stay ill

Most ill people need care, love and attention to help them back to health; alcoholics don't. Alcoholism is an illness in which sympathy and protective kindness can kill.

Most people try to 'cure their alcoholic' by helping them. They help them with jobs, they help them with their families, they help them with living accommodation. They take them to doctors and psychiatrists. They buy things for them. They give them treats. They try and talk about underlying problems. They talk about stress and a thousand other futile solutions.

And the alcoholics may co-operate with this. They promise that of course they will stop drinking or they will cut it down. If only they had a new situation, if their wives stopped nagging, if their children did better at school, if they had a better job, if their bosses got off their backs.

Sometimes they manage to stay off the alcohol or cut it down for a few weeks, even months – and then they go back on it again.

All this 'helping' allows the alcoholics to escape the consequences of their drinking. It helps the alcoholics to stay ill.

Letting the alcoholic suffer the consequences

Letting the alcoholic suffer the consequences is something that people find very hard to understand; they think that perhaps it's cruel, unfeeling and hard. But turn it round the other way. What is going to happen if you go on making excuses, go on letting them off the hook? The illness just progresses.

Intervention

Families really can do something to help and this is what we call intervention, or tough love.

John's wife, Susan, had developed a drinking problem. Each evening when he came home from work he saw the tell-tale signs. For a long time she was not apparently drunk, in the usual sense, but she looked bleary and her clothes began to become a little untidy. She frequently lost her temper and the children would stay out of the way and spend most of their time in their room.

As her drinking increased John became more and more desperate. He tried everything to get her to look at the problem. He begged, he pleaded, he threatened, he cajoled, he bought things for her, he withdrew sex, he gave her presents – anything and everything to try and control her behaviour. But nothing worked.

A friend who knew about his problem suggested that he went to Al-anon, the family part of Alcoholics Anonymous, and there he found that if he stopped doing things for her, he stopped picking up the pieces, he stopped making excuses for her – that in fact her drinking behaviour would come to a head.

This is exactly what he did, and she found that without his help and support she couldn't cope. Her drinking got worse and eventually she came to him for help.

He also sat down with the children and explained to them that Mummy was ill but she wasn't bad or weak and that they were not to accept her lies and excuses for not getting the dinner and not getting their clothes ready for school. And so the children, too, intervened in the illness.

One day at his office John had a call from Susan: 'I can't stand it any more. Help me.' And at this point she started to recover.

As long as he had, in a sense, enabled her to continue drinking by over-protecting her she would have gone on drinking for ever.

Breaking the denial syndrome

It is very unusual for alcoholics to seek help unless there is no other alternative. The people most able to force them to look at their drink problem are their families, their friends or their employers.

Alcoholics are usually unable to recognise that they need help, and this is called denial. To put it very simply, denial is the view taken that 'My drinking is not really that bad', even though everybody else can see that it is a disaster. Everyone around can see the progression of the drinking and the damage it is causing.

The solution is to use a crisis which the drinking creates so that the drinker has no alternative but to seek help. This is called intervention and it is best done in a caring but firm manner.

Sometimes it has to go as far as the non-drinking partner in a marriage saying, 'Either you will do something about your drinking or I am going to seek a separation. I need to salvage myself and the children.'

If the alcoholic is a child the parents usually have to say, 'We are not prepared to support you or have you in the home and pick up the pieces unless you get help and stay sober in Alcoholics Anonymous.'

At work a boss or a supervisor or personnel manager who has been noticing the deterioration in the performance of an employee can make a detailed history of what is going on and present it to the person he suspects has a drinking problem. The best approach is to say: 'You have been valued in this firm for years and I know that you can continue to be so if you get help with your drinking problem. Otherwise we cannot keep you. You have had endless polite warnings, we want you to be well, we want you to stay with the firm, but you have to make the choice between your drinking and your work.'

In each case there must be a commitment to follow through on the warning. If the drinking continues the solicitor must be seen, the child must leave home, and the personnel manager must dismiss the employee, otherwise the option becomes meaningless. It must be made clear that abstinence is an expected goal and that a change towards more responsible behaviour must occur through treatment and/or involvement in the self-help group of Alcoholics Anonymous.

In our experience, despite the fact that the alcoholic is forced to seek help, the outcome is usually successful. It is very common, years later, to hear from a recovering person, 'If only someone had forced me to face myself years before, I wouldn't have wasted so much of my life or hurt so many.' One of the saddest aspects of this illness is that usually the drinking alcoholic will only grudgingly accept help when there is no other choice.

Letting the alcoholic know how you feel

The chances are that the illness first shows itself at home among the family. At work and socially, the alcoholic seems to behave acceptably for a number of years. The brunt of the bad behaviour is borne by those with whom he or she lives. The alcoholic is the street angel and the home devil. We have said that nagging, threatening, coaxing, pleading with the alcoholic is a waste of time but that doesn't mean that you should sit like Patience on a monument doing nothing – far from it.

Let the alcoholic know how you feel. Tell the alcoholic clearly and directly when he or she is reasonably sober if you are upset, hurt, angry or afraid.

Shouting or screaming will simply mean the message isn't heard. If you lose your temper or weep all the time he or she will use this as an excuse to drink more. But, tell it like it is, in a caring way: 'I was really angry last night when you came home drunk and frightened the children.' Say how you feel when the alcoholic can hear it – perhaps the morning after. Say it in a firm, caring way and say it just once. When you have said it, carry on with what you are doing, otherwise the alcoholic will draw you into an argument or debate and you will find that *you* will end up apologising – manipulated yet again.

This technique achieves two things: it confronts the alcoholic with the consequences of getting drunk (and remember that alcoholics may not remember what they have done, especially if they are suffering from alcoholic amnesia). And it allows you to express your feelings. It shows the alcoholic that you cannot go on being used or abused. It stops arguments. Alcoholics are brilliant at twisting words to suit themselves. A good fight allows them to put you in the wrong and to ignore the fact that their behaviour started it all.

Tough love

This way of acting is called tough love and *tough love means stopping trying to rescue the alcoholic and starting to let him or her suffer*. Because only by suffering the painful consequences of dependence will the alcoholic begin to realise that he or she has a problem.

It is just like the tough love that you practise with a child. If you say to your six-year-old that he should go to bed at seven o'clock the child may wheedle, may have a tantrum, may sulk, may try playing one parent off against the other; if you back down and let him stay up you could bring up a spoilt child. He learns by experience that you don't mean what you say, you don't back up your words with actions, so he stops listening to the words.

It's just the same with an alcoholic. Practising tough love doesn't come easily; many families are so frantic with anxiety and fear they simply won't pause to listen to advice – they go on trying to control their alcoholics. They say they want the alcoholics to stop drinking but their actions are showing the opposite. Through their actions they actually reward them for drinking by finding accommodation, fixing jobs, paying fines, doing their work at home for them, mowing the lawn for them and in general giving them all their attention. In this way you help the alcoholic stay drinking.

To help the alcoholic you have to help yourself

Many families are so concentrated on looking at the drinker's behaviour and at his drinking that they don't have time to look at what's happening to them. As we have seen in Chapters 4 and 5, they become solely fixed on the sick person and they often become sick physically and emotionally themselves.

But remember, to help the alcoholic, you have to help yourself, because:

1. *The family suffers more than the alcoholic*. Alcoholics avoid emotional pain by simply getting drunk. They don't feel the emotional turmoil going on around them.

2. *Alcoholics may actually thrive in such circumstances*. When other members of the family are behaving in such a sick way, their own inappropriate behaviour doesn't show up so much. They need not face themselves because they can point to the distorted behaviour of everyone else. It gives them an excellent excuse to go on drinking.

3. *If family members get emotionally too damaged they won't be there*

when they are needed – at the moment when the alcoholic decides that perhaps he wants to do something about his drinking. Families who have an alcoholic need to stop giving all their attention to the drinker.

4. *Making the sick person the focus of attention is bad for him* – it encourages him to manipulate those around him. Start practising emotional detachment. If the alcoholic is angry or unhappy it doesn't mean you have to have the same feelings.

Getting on with your own life

Don't let the emotional mess of the alcoholic's life spill over into yours. Start focusing on your own life. Take your rest. Go out and enjoy yourself. Meet friends. Go to the cinema, theatre, parties and so on, just as you would do if everything was all right. Even partners of alcoholics who may be financially in difficult circumstances can do something they enjoy – even if it's only going to meet a friend for a cup of tea or taking a walk in the park, or watching some TV.

What's good for you is good for the alcoholic.

Make a conscious effort to rebuild your life. Repair your social life. You may well not want to share this with your alcoholic because alcoholics are not much fun to have around.

Joining Al-anon

By joining Al-anon, the family part of Alcoholics Anonymous, and attending their meetings, you will receive the love and encouragement that you need, from people in the same boat. The phone numbers are in Appendix 2.

These self-help organisations are made up of families and friends who know what it is like to have an alcoholic in their life. There are mothers, fathers, wives, husbands, partners, lovers, sisters, brothers and friends. They know what you are going through.

To somebody full of guilt, anger and despair, these meetings may seem a bit strange at first and that is why it is very important to go to several meetings before making up your mind whether to let them help you. When you first go it seems a bit simplistic and you don't feel they really understand how bad your problem is. Keep going – you will find that they do.

It is vital to start getting help from Al-anon before the position gets totally disastrous.

Checklist for family intervention

Many of the ideas we have put forward in this chapter may seem new, but the principles do work. If you follow these suggestions you will minimise the damage that alcoholism wreaks on those around the alcoholic and you will give your alcoholic a better chance. Here's what to do:

1. *Join Al-anon* and get support and encouragement from others in a similar position.

2. *Stop blaming yourself* – you didn't make your alcoholic an alcoholic. Take no notice when the alcoholic blames you – he would, wouldn't he? That way he has a reason or an excuse to go on drinking.

3. *Stop trying to rescue him* – you can't control his drinking and you can't cure it. Checking up on him, trying to control his intake, trying to control his life will not work and it just punishes you.

4. *Stop trying to understand the alcoholic* – pondering the underlying reasons wastes energy and gets nowhere. Experts don't even know the answer to this. Stop asking the unanswerable 'Why?' and start focusing on treatment.

5. *Stop threatening, nagging, coaxing, bullying, bribing or lecturing* – instead of this, start letting the alcoholic know how you feel in a caring way.

6. *Let the alcoholic suffer the consequences of his own drinking.* That means letting him or her go downhill. For only by standing back in this way is there any hope that he will stop.

7. *Start offering the alcoholic choices* – 'If you want help I will back you all the way; if you want to stay sick you are on your own.'

8. *Get on with your life.* Look after your own needs, feelings and emotions, do things to make yourself happy. What's good for you is good for the alcoholic.

9. *Start rebuilding your family.* Remember you have children and friends who need your time and love. They often get neglected when you are concentrating everything on the alcoholic. Minimise the damage to yourself and the family.

10. *Learn about this illness.* Once you do so you can stop all that fretting about 'Is he or isn't he an alcoholic?' and 'How much does he drink?' You can also stop listening to all that well-meaning advice from the ignorant, who sometimes include journalists, TV personalities and, alas, even some well-intentioned doctors and social workers who have been deceived by alcoholics. And instead you can start listening to people with personal experience or specialised training.

PART FOUR

For the Alcoholic

7

Are You an Alcoholic?

Since alcohol is obviously harmful to people, why on earth do they go on drinking? Outsiders are constantly baffled by the persistence with which alcoholics go on drinking – no matter how often they are warned, lectured, threatened, helped and even 'treated'.

This persistence is at the heart of the illness which affects alcoholics – the illness of chemical dependence.

Alcoholics are not bad people, no matter how bad their behaviour becomes. They are sick people. Dependence is an illness of the body and the mind, most of all an illness of the emotions, either deadening or exaggerating them.

After all, what sane person would go on drinking when his children are frightened, his wife wants to leave and his job is on the line? The alcoholic does.

Denial

Here is the mystery of dependence. Alcoholics are literally the last people to see what the illness is doing to them. If they do, they are blind to the obvious way to recover. This is the mental side of the illness. The concept of stopping drinking altogether seems to be terrifying.

It is an illness which tells the sufferer that he or she hasn't got the illness.

An alcoholic is characterised by denial. He or she seems unable or unwilling to admit the problem.

There is also an element of ethical deterioration – what the recovering alcoholic sometimes calls the spiritual side of the illness. An alcoholic's behaviour becomes worse and worse as the illness progresses.

How to recognise alcoholism

If you are an alcoholic or if you love an alcoholic you need to recognise the illness. Blindness to the progressive indications of the disease are brought about by the misconceptions we have already talked about. If you are looking for the gross behaviour often portrayed in books and films, you are looking at the end stages of the illness. If you are thinking of an alcoholic as a bag-lady or someone lying on the Embankment under a dirty raincoat covered in newspapers, then you will not recognise the illness in your husband or wife as it begins.

Like any other illness, the earlier you recognise and treat it the better. The later you treat it the harder it is to recover. That is why it is so important to recognise the early symptoms. To begin with, the signs of dependence are as subtle and illusive as a rainbow. There is little consistency.

Little trivial things start to happen: forgotten appointments, promises broken (mainly to children), jobs started and not completed, work good one day and not the next.

Sadly people see this as irresponsible behaviour and imma-turity, and often do not connect it with drinking occasions. Unpredictability in mood becomes noticeable. The moods do not seem to be related to events, which becomes very confusing for family and friends. Progressively, little things start to slide and people around the alcoholic begin to feel uncomfortable and don't know why.

Men are worse off than women in the recognition stakes as there is an expectation that men will drink, particularly when young. It is almost as if it is part of becoming a man and therefore acceptable.

Alcoholics show definite and increasing signs of their depen-dence. Here are some of the symptoms.

Lack of control

There is progressively less and less control over your drinking. This means that you are unable to predict with any certainty what will happen after the first drink. There is a random nature to the drinking and an impulsiveness that seems totally illogical. You may have just one or two drinks and be perfectly all right, but you may go on to be embarrassing or even disgusting. *The alcohol is controlling you rather than you controlling the alcohol.*

In the long run you cannot consistently reduce the amount you take or regulate it when you wish.

Ask an alcoholic to have just two drinks a day with no excuses and no justifications for taking more, such as weddings or going to the races; they come back and say to you, 'Ah, but this was a special occasion.' They *could* have done it had they wanted to! But the point is, they can't and they didn't. They may fully intend to do so but seem to be unable to do it. They intend to reduce the amount yet don't seem to be able to manage it. The behaviour becomes more and more unpredictable once the drinking begins.

Many times you will hear an alcoholic say, 'I'll just have *a* drink' or 'I'll just have a *couple* of drinks'; the intention is to drink no more than that but it never really happens.

Surreptitious behaviour

Alcoholics tend to be devious about their use of alcohol. They will often lie repeatedly, even idiotically to those around them. They will hide their drink towards the end stages of the disease.

Women particularly hide things around the house, in the laundry cupboard, under the mattress, under the bed, under the stairs, in the wellingtons by the door, outside in the garage. Anywhere, so that nobody will know when they are drinking or how much they are drinking.

Men will often carry a flat half-bottle in a brief case or in the bottom drawer of their desk just in case they need it. They seem to have an ever growing fear of being without alcohol, and yet outwardly they may be smart, well dressed, have a good job, look good and sound good. But gradually things start to slide.

Other kinds of deviousness appear, like buying bottles in different supermarkets or off-licences.

Alcoholics surround themselves with other heavy drinkers. It's so much nicer to be able to say, 'Oh well, Joe drinks so much more than me – now he is a *real* alcoholic.'

This surreptitious behaviour is often accompanied by shame,

guilt and fear. Women alcoholics, in particular, suffer from the anguish of their drinking being found out. There is still a double standard. If you are a man and you drink a hell of a lot, you are a hell of a guy, if you are a woman you are a loser.

Mental obsession

Alcohol takes over the mind of the alcoholic and life begins to centre around drinking. Great effort is put into making sure that drink is always available. You make excuses for drinking occasions, so that you can drink openly and publicly and no one will take note of it. Alcoholics sometimes show an obsession with drink and talk endlessly about how much and when and with whom – it can be incredibly boring.

Alcoholism is a chemical addiction

Some people don't like the word alcoholic. They feel that this is a stigma in itself. But there is no point in using polite names for an illness which is so destructive, which can be terminal and which causes untold harm to the people around the alcoholic.

It doesn't matter what drug you are on, whether it's alcohol, tranquillisers, heroin, cocaine, they can all create dependency. Alcohol is just one of these drugs. It is important to remember that there is no point in getting off alcohol to transfer to another dependence on another flavour. It never works. If you try and substitute any other drug for alcohol, you will either very quickly become dependent on that drug or return to drink.

Alcoholics are just ethyl-alcohol addicts under a different name and what is so dangerous is that they are drinking a legally available drug. The illness is chemical dependence.

That's why there is only one answer to chemical dependence – complete abstinence from any kind of mood-altering drug. No alcohol, no tranquillisers, no cocaine and no heroin.

This may sound a very tough approach. This is a very tough illness. **It's a killer illness and half-measures get you nowhere.** You don't even get half well from half-measures. You stay totally ill. In the long run offering an easy answer, like 'Just cut it down, you'll be fine,' is not being kind to the alcoholic. Substituting drugs isn't kind to the alcoholic because it doesn't work. The only kindness to suffering alcoholics is to help them get sober and well, not to enable them to stay sick.

Definition of sober

To be sober means to be abstinent from alcohol and from any other mood-altering chemical, and to be happy *not* drinking.

Getting honest

Sally was a nice girl from a Scottish village who all her young life had wanted to be a nurse. She got into hospital and did her training and while she was there she had, as she called it, a good time. She worked hard, she played hard, she went out to the pubs with other students and other nurses. Okay, so she drank a little too much now and then. It wasn't that bad.

She qualified, started working as a staff nurse and very shortly afterwards met her boyfriend, Bill, whom she married eighteen months later.

Gradually, as the years went by, she found that she started looking forward to a drink when she got home. Sometimes she would have more than one and sometimes more than two. Then her husband would question her about it, which would make her upset and angry.

She was promoted in the hospital to a job where there was a lot of responsibility and she was a bit frightened of this.

She thought to herself one day, 'I'll just take a couple of Valium, that will make me feel better.' So she did. Within a year Sally was taking Valium daily and she had built up her drinking to three or four large drinks every evening when she got home. This created rows and fights; her husband got totally fed up with her behaviour. It never occurred to either of them that she had a growing drinking problem.

About a year later when Sally got pregnant, her husband said to her, 'Don't you think you should stop drinking now that you're pregnant?' Sally answered, 'No, that's all right. I can handle it, I only have one or two. It won't hurt the baby.' Several months later she had a baby and after two years she had another.

By the time Sally came into treatment, her children were six and eight years old; she was drinking between a half and a whole bottle of vodka a day and taking sometimes between 30 and 80 milligrammes of Valium – and she was still working. Because she was drinking so **much she didn't** sleep very well. She started topping up with a few sleeping pills.

Sally was only in her early thirties when she came for help with her alcoholism, shattered by what she had done to her family, terrified of the fear in her children's faces. But hers is a typical story. Most alcoholics are intelligent, most are working, most are married and most have children, and alcoholism creates havoc in their lives. For years Sally couldn't see that her drinking was getting out of control. Her husband recognised it, he told her, her mother told her, even her doctor told her. She denied it.

This is an illness which tells you that you haven't got it, so it is very difficult for you to see the truth.

You feel that you are different. You are not really alcoholic. You just drink a little too much now and then. You start justifying a drink. Maybe it's because your wife doesn't care or your parents spoilt you, or you don't have a job, or your job is too much for you. Your family had too much money or not enough. Excuses, excuses and excuses. These aren't reasons – they are cop-outs.

To get well you have to be honest. You have to listen to that voice within you which is still there. It may be only a small voice but it's telling you that you are ill and that you need help.

Honesty is what gets the alcoholic well, the courage to be honest, the courage to look at what is really happening because of the progressive drinking.

Are you an alcoholic?

The simplest way to decide is to ask yourself what drink is doing to your life. Not how much you drink or when you drink or how you drink or who you drink with. But is it causing harm in any of the following areas of your life and yet you continue to drink.

1. Health.
2. Personal life.
3. Family life.
4. Social life.
5. Work or occupation. People who do not do paid employment should ask themselves if alcohol is affecting their housework, their voluntary work or any other work of this kind.
6. Finance. Look for debts, over-commitments, too much spent on alcohol.
7. Ethical behaviour. That means do you break your own standards when you drink?

These are the main areas in which alcohol may be giving you

problems. If you are alcoholic you may find it difficult to see the problems so here are some more detailed questions.

Is alcohol causing problems in your life?

Try to answer these questions honestly:

1. *Have you found over the years that you need more alcohol to get the same effect?*

Did you find when you first started drinking that you had a pretty hard head for alcohol and could drink quite a lot without showing it? Perhaps you were the one who put everybody else to bed, but nowadays you need more drink to get the same effect.

2. *At any time in your drinking, have there been periods when you don't remember what happened?*

Alcoholics have these memory lapses, but they function, they talk, they maybe carry on a business deal or go to a party. But they can't remember afterwards exactly what happened, what they said or sometimes how they got home. This can last for a few minutes or in severe cases even over twenty-four hours. As the illness gets worse, time difficulties and blackouts, as these memory lapses are called, increase in number and become more unpredictable.

3. *Have you ever sneaked a drink?*

For instance having a quiet drink before you go out, without the wife knowing. Or sneaking off to your room where maybe you have a bottle hidden. Or perhaps, before you have to do some business deal, tanking up to give yourself confidence.

4. *Are you preoccupied with drinking?*

Alcoholics talk about what and when they drank, the pubs they know, the drinking occasions. Other interests start to slip away. Maybe you used to be very interested in sports or the theatre or music and you suddenly begin to realise that you haven't done any of these things for years because they interfered with your drinking.

5. *Do you drink more and more in a hurry?*

You realise the need for the first drink and you can't wait to get the first drink down. Do you get into a bad mood if you can't drink when and where and how you want?

6. *Are you reluctant to talk about your drinking?*

If the wife or the children or the parents have said things about your drinking, do you try and avoid the subject? Alcoholics often get angry if people suggest they drink too much.

7. *Do you sometimes lose control after the first drink?*

Alcoholics often tell themselves, 'I'll just have a drink or two,' and they fully intend to do that. But on some occasions, not every occasion, control goes and you find yourself drunk, having yet another row or maybe falling flat on your face. Are you the first at a party and the last to leave? Are your friends telling you that you are becoming embarrassing? This loss of control may not occur every time but the results of taking the first drink become increasingly unpredictable.

8. *Do you find yourself making up excuses or alibis, or even downright lies, to explain your drinking behaviour?*

Alcoholics are very adept at this. 'Well I had this wedding to go to' or 'I had this party' or 'I had to entertain this important customer'. Anything and everything to justify going on drinking.

9. *Have your family or friends begun to say anything about your drinking?*

They are embarrassed, concerned, anxious, they make suggestions like 'Maybe you should go and talk to a doctor' or 'Maybe you should cut down'. There are rows, they ask for promises, they threaten and beg you to look at your drinking.

10. *Have you begun to spend too much money and be extravagant?*

This kind of grandiosity keeps the alcoholic feeling somewhat superior to everyone else. Alcoholics may spend money recklessly as if there were no tomorrow. They have to be the big man, controlling everything and everybody, even to how much other people drink around them. They often force drinks on other people who don't want them.

11. *Are you unable to take questions about or criticism of your behaviour?*

This over-sensitivity increases in the alcoholic, who becomes very touchy and over-reacts to the slightest comment.

12. *Do you have times when you feel remorseful, guilty or ashamed about your behaviour when you are drinking?*

These feelings of unease can occur at any time, even when there seems to be no apparent reason. Under the influence of this remorse, resolutions to give up are made, only to be broken. In the end some alcoholics feel nothing and show no moral sense at all. In their drinking they are just looking for release from their own pain rather than for any form of pleasure.

13. *Do you have spells when you stop drinking?*

Many alcoholics tell themselves they are not alcoholics because they can stop. 'I stopped for Lent', 'I stop for a fortnight a year just to let my body have a rest'. All this really means is stopping to get fit enough to drink again. Any drinker who feels that they have to stop for a period of time to get well should look seriously at their drinking behaviour. You can delude yourself this way that you are not dependent. For it is a myth that you cannot stop when you are an alcoholic. Any alcoholic can stop for a time. It's the way they start again, and again, and again that shows that they are dependent. Sometimes periods of abstinence at home or at health farms or clinics are a way of trying to control the drinking. After drying out, getting better physically the alcoholic tells himself that there isn't a problem.

14. *Have you changed the pattern of the way you drink?*

Have you moved from one flavour to another? Have you stopped spirits and gone on to the wine as a way to control your intake? Alcoholics try and change even the flavour of their drinks switching from gin to vodka to whisky. Women particularly drink vodka thinking it won't smell. And that is another myth!

15. *Have you lost any friends you had before the drinking became a problem?*

Have childhood friends, close friends or work friends begun to drop out of your life? Do they ask you round for a meal less often? Do they come round to you less often? Are you, in fact, becoming quite isolated?

16. *Has alcohol affected your work?*

This is usually the last area to be affected: after all, work is the source of money to buy drink. Those who are employed may work for many years before their workmates get fed up with their drinking or their supervisor tells them something has to change or they get sacked. If you are self-employed you can kid yourself for a long time that there isn't a problem. Men cover up for their mates and tell themselves that it is loyalty. In fact this is a betrayal of loyalty and can kill people.

17. *Has the attitude of your friends and family worsened?*

Family and friends who were once anxious and caring about your drinking now begin to get pretty fed up and pretty angry. Alcoholics may now find they are thrown out of the family home and discarded by friends.

18. *Have you had any kind of medical, hospital or residential treatment for your alcoholism?*

Alcoholics, as the disease becomes more chronic, begin the round of medical establishments. Sometimes they are treated, other times they may just be dried out. Sometimes they mistakenly are diagnosed as depressive or as having some other mental or physical illness. These are quite convenient for alcoholics, who can then convince themselves, 'I am only drinking because I'm depressed so if I treat my depression then I can drink.' Of course alcohol is a depressant drug and it makes all your emotions depressed.

19. *Have you tried changing your job, your friend, your wife, your home or your country to escape your problem?*

In an attempt to escape the growing pain of their problem, alcoholics start changing their environment. They change jobs to avoid stress. They think that stress makes them drink. But it doesn't make any difference because in fact it is the drinking that has created the stress. They may change partners, they may try living in a new area, they may go abroad and hope this will do the trick. They do not realise that the problem, the illness, is within them and that wherever they go they take it with them.

20. *Do you make sure that alcohol is always available?*

Do you make sure there is always alcohol in the house? Do you buy more just in case you run out? If you finish a bottle in the evening are you panicky at the thought of what you are going to have tomorrow?

21. *Do you use alcohol to get you going?*

Towards the end of their illness, some alcoholics are drinking in the morning just to get themselves together. They wake up panicky, physically shaky. Their hands shake, their stomach shakes. Just a drink or two will get them together enough to function or to reach the office without anybody noticing the shakes.

22. *Do you do things under the influence of alcohol you would not do when you were not drinking?*

The alcoholic's behaviour seems to show signs of ethical deterioration. Often this is a direct result of the drinking. But sometimes as the disease progresses, the deterioration will even occur when the alcoholic is away from alcohol. They are not necessarily very dramatic signs but they are enough to make you uncomfortable. You lie to your loved ones. You may fiddle your expenses or the housekeeping money or steal money out of your husband's wallet when he is asleep. You may run up bills at the supermarket or at the shop that you cannot pay. You may have shoplifted. You may have mugged people. You may sleep with people you do not even like. You may have sex for money. By the end most alcoholics show an utter disregard for themselves and others, and their self-worth hits rock bottom.

23. *Are you drinking more or less continuously now?*

You always have a drink or a bottle of whisky within reach and are terrified if there isn't one.

Alcoholics suffer from fear which has no reason. There may be unexplained attacks of panic and anxiety and an appalling sense of 'impending doom'.

How to use the questionnaire

This is not a formal questionnaire and there are no points to score. However, its questions indicate the progressive nature of alcoholism.

Did *any* of the questions relate to you? Because if any of them did, you may be dependent on alcohol. The more questions that apply, the worse the progression of your alcoholism. Remember, an alcoholic is somebody who goes on using alcohol even though it is causing problems.

This questionnaire can also be used by families and friends who suspect someone they love may have a problem with alcohol.

8

Deciding to Come Off Drink

If you decide you have become dependent, do not be disheartened. Facing the reality of alcoholism is the first step towards getting well.

The earlier that you do decide to stop drinking, the easier your recovery.

The dangers of delay

Sadly many alcoholics feel that there is no urgency about stopping and they find excuses to put it off. Many times you hear the phrase, 'I'll quit tomorrow.' The tragedy for many people is that tomorrow never comes. They tell themselves, 'I am not that bad, I don't drink any more than Joe Bloggs, so I can't have a problem.' These delaying tactics mean they just become iller and their recovery becomes more difficult. Alcoholics who take this approach are gambling with their lives, for this illness can kill.

Look at it this way. If a woman finds a tiny lump in her breast, she immediately visits her doctor in case it's cancer. The smaller it is the easier it is to treat and the more likely she is to recover. But if she delays, telling herself, 'It's not really cancer, it's not that bad, the lump will go away,' it won't be long before that cancer has grown and grown, and she may lose her life. This can happen to those who delay getting help for alcoholism.

Here are some of the excuses that alcoholics give:

1. I haven't lost my job.
2. I haven't lost the love of my family.
3. I haven't lost my friends.
4. I haven't lost my health.

Have another look at those excuses for remaining ill. Are they that good? One way to put them into perspective is to add one little word '*yet*' at the end of each one. Now look at them: You haven't lost your job – yet. You have not lost the love of your family – yet. You haven't lost your friends – yet. You have not lost your health – yet.

With that little extra word these excuses for doing nothing look different. These excuses are like warnings. So every time you find yourself using an excuse, add that little word 'yet'. It might save your life.

Hitting rock bottom

When you feel you just can't go on any longer, you have hit rock bottom. It feels like the worst place in the world. Everybody has a slightly different experience of hitting this rock bottom, but most alcoholics agree that until they have this feeling, they are not forced to change. When at last they feel that they can't go on any more, then, finally, they are willing to get help.

Ken's rock bottom

Ken's rock bottom came when his wife left him. He had been a very successful engineer for many years and had had a succession of good jobs. He had been in the most recent firm for some twelve years and had been highly thought of until very recently, but his job was beginning to slip.

For years his home life had been hell. He had come home every evening, gone to the pub on the way home, hit the bottle and continued drinking. Then he would start getting into fights with his wife and raging at the children. He even accused his wife of having an affair, which was the last thing on her mind: she was far too upset with what was happening to her marriage. She pleaded and she wept. He made promises which he broke continually, but it wasn't until she had the courage to go to a solicitor and tell him what had happened and serve Ken with papers for a separation that he realised how serious his problem was.

That was his rock bottom and that's what brought him into treatment. But he was bewildered, angry, upset and frightened, and he had no real recognition of how bad his behaviour had been.

Asking for help

Very few alcoholics manage to give up alcohol alone – that is, without some kind of support. Drink has been so important in their lives that when they stop there is a great gap in their way of life and something has to take its place. They may in fact have stopped many times, but without help it gets worse. Drinking gets worse. When they stop, the withdrawals get worse and then there is nothing but a big black hole.

Alcoholics who just try to carry on without putting anything in the place of alcohol eventually fail. Sooner or later most go back to drinking. After all, if alcoholism is an illness, it needs some kind of extra care. If you went into hospital for an appendix removal it would be madness to discharge yourself directly you came out of surgery. You simply wouldn't be well enough to go back into normal life. Besides you can't take out the stitches yourself. It is just the same with alcoholism: you are going to need proper after-care.

So if you want to get well you are going to need help. It is not enough to know you need it – you have got to ask for it. The sooner you make this move the better.

Alcoholism is a subtle and cunning disease, and it will try to lure you into false optimism and all kinds of reasons for not doing what will get you well.

If you are an alcoholic with a family who has not yet given up hope you may well have had offers of help already. They may have told you about clinics that will help you or offered to go with you to get help, or perhaps you know an alcoholic who has got sober in AA. Perhaps they have told you about it and are offering you help. Maybe it is time you accepted this help which you so indignantly refused before. Maybe you are embarrassed or angry at the thought that you are having to change your mind and tell them that you need help.

Don't let false pride, shame or fear stop your chances. If you know where help is available, grab it.

The best kind of help is from other recovering alcoholics who know what it is like to stop drinking. They have learned how to live life without alcohol. You will find them in Alcoholics Anonymous.

Alcoholics Anonymous

Alcoholics Anonymous is a self-help organisation which has flourished since 1935.

AA discovered a secret which has revolutionised the treatment of alcoholism. The best person to help a drinking alcoholic is usually another alcoholic who has discovered how to stay sober. There are many AA meetings all over the country and all over the world. You will find AA in most large towns – they are usually in the phone book. So help is always readily available. AA holds meetings in church halls, hospitals, clinics, homes and offices – in fact, anywhere where the rent is cheap. There are no dues or fees.

If you decide you want help, all you have to do is ring their number, and they will put local members in touch with you or tell you where the nearest meeting is.

Meetings vary but a fairly typical meeting will usually have a secretary and a speaker, and this speaker will say something about his life and particularly about how he recovered from alcoholism. Other alcoholics at the meeting will join in, adding their own comments and telling something about their own experience. Newcomers aren't required to speak, but they can if they want to.

AA membership is for everybody who wants to stop drinking. As the preamble to every AA meeting puts it, the only requirement is a desire to stop drinking.

There is little formal advice or counselling given. **Meetings mainly concentrate on sharing personal experiences and problems, giving hope, and helping recovery.**

It is extremely important to remember one vital fact: an alcoholic is never cured. Stopping drinking is only the first step towards recovery. You need the maintenance of continued AA to stay off alcohol. It is rather like having diabetes; it is an illness from which people can recover quite simply by taking insulin but if they stop taking it they will relapse back into the active phase of the disease. Insulin helps them to recover and lead a normal life, but it isn't a cure. In the same way AA will help you to recover from your alcoholism but it is not a once-for-all cure. Most alcoholics have some difficulties getting started on a sober life. **AA offers**

guidance, support and discipline, helping alcoholics to accept their disease and to keep in touch with it, so that they do not lapse into wishful thinking that they can drink again.

Getting a doctor to help

If you are attending AA you may find that is all you need to do. Many thousands of men and women have recovered from alcoholism in this way without further help. However, it is possible that you will need professional help at the time when you are getting off alcohol. Withdrawal from alcohol can be difficult and dangerous – more so if you are using tranquillisers as well. You should ask for medical help at that stage of your recovery.

It is not always easy to find a doctor who will understand our view of alcoholism. Many may tell you just to cut down or to substitute other drugs. The sensible thing to do is to ask a doctor to withdraw you over a short period of time, with a drug that is very similar to alcohol. It should be given in a reducing dose for five or six days to get you safely off the alcohol so that you will not have the physical withdrawal effects (which will be described later).

Some alcoholics may need to go into hospital or into clinics – and some of these are better than others. Take the advice of people in AA who have been through this experience or ask somebody there to recommend a good hospital or clinic. They usually know the ones where you will get good treatment from staff who understand withdrawal and will not put you on long-term substitute drugs which will then lead to endless trouble and possible future addiction.

There are several hospitals and clinics available that have a positive and caring approach to the alcoholic and which also understand the twelve-step programme of AA. For advice on this there is a list in Appendix 2.

9

How to Stop Drinking

Stopping drinking is simple. It isn't easy but it is simple. Anybody who really wants to stop drinking can do so. Thousands of people are living examples of how it has been done and of the happiness that results from a life free from alcohol.

You can do it too. You've probably done it, many, many times. With all those past attempts to stop drinking behind you, you are probably frightened of what will happen if you try and fail again.

Put out of your mind the idea that you cannot live without alcohol. In fact you can live very well and be happier than you were when drinking. People who develop a drinking problem are very fearful of life without a drink, or think they cannot be normal without a drink. You feel you cannot function without a drink, but in fact you can. Millions do, and you can be one of them.

Physical withdrawal symptoms

First of all you should learn about the withdrawal symptoms from coming off alcohol. Is it dangerous? Do you need help? Many alcoholics can, in fact, just stop. They feel very uncomfortable but they can do it. If you have stopped previously without any serious side-effects then it is probably safe just to stop.

There are, however, withdrawal symptoms that are physical

and emotional, and you should be aware of these. For most alcoholics who have been drinking heavily and regularly it is wise to have some medical advice if you are deciding to stop drinking.

Most people when they stop have feelings of discomfort, shakiness and sickness; some become sweaty and get the cramps. Sometimes they feel agitated and restless, and their concentration goes. Most people experience some insomnia, and the first three days are the worst.

With most alcoholics this is all that will happen to you but if you have really been punishing the bottle for many years then it can be a worse condition called DTs or delirium tremens (see p. 20). This is the name given to really violent withdrawal attacks which are sometimes accompanied by seeing or hearing things that are not there. Alcohol withdrawal fits can also follow. This is a seizure rather like that seen in epileptics. That is why alcoholics should have some medical help in withdrawal. If these fits are not prevented or dealt with properly they can be fatal.

It's very important to have a back-up system while you are going through withdrawal and during continuing recovery. Get to Alcoholics Anonymous and initially try to attend their meetings daily if possible.

A week off work will probably help you in the first days of your recovery but get back to normal living as soon as possible.

If you are on more than one drug – in other words, if you are mixing your alcohol with, for instance, tranquillisers – it is essential that you get help from a doctor. If you are habitually using alcohol with barbiturates or with benzodiazepine tranquillisers you must take measures to avoid serious withdrawal, by withdrawing *only* under medical supervision.

Psychological withdrawal symptoms

The psychological withdrawal symptoms can in fact be more painful than the physical. All alcoholics will get some psychological symptoms when they stop using alcohol. These are uncomfortable but not dangerous.

1. *Cravings for drink.* These may be constant throughout the day or may hit you at odd moments. They may feel overwhelming but they aren't. Think of them as a kind of trick that alcohol is playing on you – it wants you as a user of alcohol. Rule number one about coming off drink is do not act on the cravings.

2. *Emotional confusion.* Mood swings are common in the first few

days. You may swing from elation to serious feelings of depression, or from happiness to rage. All kinds of unpleasant feelings emerge as the alcohol leaves your system. Fear and anxiety are common. These emotions are painful but in themselves cannot hurt you. Keep reminding yourself that they will not last for ever and that you can manage today without a drink to relieve them.

3. *Small aches and pains*. These have normally been blotted out by alcohol; now they can hit you with surprising force. Alcoholics are not used to physical pain because it has generally been anaesthetised by the drink. Pains like these are a sign that you are at last in touch with your own body.

4. *Agitation, restlessness and fatigue*. The mind seems unable to concentrate and the body unable to relax, yet you may feel absolutely exhausted at the same time. Thinking is unclear and you may be unable to settle on anything.

5. *Fear*. Many alcoholics have a feeling of indefinable fear that is almost overwhelming. There are real fears too. You may be terrified that you will not be able to stay off the alcohol, frantic with the thought that you may not be able to resist it. On the other hand, you may fear a life without a drink. That is why it is a good idea to spend as much time as possible in AA. Stay in the company of recovering alcoholics as much as you can or with friends and family who will support you and understand what you are going through.

6. *Insomnia*. Several nights of sleeplessness are common when you first come off alcohol. You may find you cannot get to sleep at all, you stay awake all the night. This is extremely unpleasant but it doesn't harm you. Nobody dies from lack of sleep. Sometimes the recovering alcoholic is hit by nightmares or drinking dreams. This can be very scary and when you wake up in the morning you are not quite sure whether it is real or not but this does pass quite rapidly.

How to cope with withdrawal symptoms

Withdrawal symptoms are very unpleasant; indeed this is often why people stay on alcohol in the first place – to avoid the withdrawal. Alcoholics are bad at living through pain because they have used the booze to escape unpleasant reality. But if you want to be well you have to learn to cope with withdrawal. You have probably done it many times before – you have stopped for a particular reason, you have stopped for Lent, you have stopped because the family have someone coming to stay – but this time you are going to stay stopped. Thousands of recovering alcoholics have discovered the principles of coping with withdrawal. If they can do it, you can do it.

1. *Craving for a drink doesn't mean you have to take it.* Live through it. It is possible to live through persistent, even continuous, craving for days if not weeks, but for most people it doesn't last this long. Later we will give you some ideas that will carry you through.

2. *Live through the feeling of discomfort.* Alcoholics are very bad, as we have said, at enduring pain, whether it is physical or emotional. They are used to blotting it out with a drink. So the trick of coming off is to learn to live through the pain, literally to endure it. This is why it is important to keep busy going into AA daily for the first few weeks. It helps to distract the mind. Comfort yourself with the thought that this discomfort will only last a few days.

3. *Talk about what you are going through.* This is another reason for going to AA meetings. The illness of alcohol dependence can partially be talked out of the system during meetings. Share your pain with others and you will find that it gets less and less.

4. *Withdrawal symptoms are a sign of recovery.* This is the good news. The using alcoholic doesn't suffer from withdrawal, only the recovering alcoholic has these discomforts. They are the first signs of the body and mind coming out of the illness. Keep remembering this. Remember too there is a lot of happiness waiting.

5. *You only have to do it once.* If you do it this time you will never have to go through it again. If you put your heart and soul into it, this bad time when you are getting sober is a once-and-for-all experience.

You can recover.

No matter how uncomfortable and painful it feels, you will recover. In the next chapter we will tell you how to get through the first few weeks of recovery.

10

The First Few Weeks Off Drink

Now stop.

Just don't take any more alcohol. Say 'No' to yourself and to your drinking friends. It is as simple as that. Concentrate with every fibre of your being on not taking the first drink.

Do it now.

If you do have to cut down at the advice of your doctor or if you have been using tranquillisers with alcohol, make sure that the next pill is the right cut-down dose as part of the programme. Tranquilliser addicts who also use alcohol will need to bear in mind that an abrupt stop, which other addicts can manage, is not necessarily suitable for them. Alcoholics, too, must remember that abruptly stopping without any medication for withdrawal can be dangerous.

The first few hours and days may not be easy. However, you will get through them if you practise the skills of AA. These are truly lifeline tricks designed to keep you clean and sober despite the pain of coming down off alcohol.

The twenty-four-hour plan

Give up alcohol just for the day. The day you are in now, or the twenty-four hours that started from your last drink. Literally everybody, every single alcoholic, can give up alcohol for a day. You may have done it many times, times when you gave up for a reason, or because you couldn't get hold of a drink, or because you were trying to keep the wife off your back, or because you were just telling yourself you wouldn't pick up another drink.

This mental trick concentrates all your mental energies where they should be, on staying off that drink *now*. It also means that you can stop worrying about tomorrow or next week or next year or how you are going to manage at the office party.

Most alcoholics cannot see themselves staying off alcohol for ever. Indeed if they think of it that way they simply become frightened, downhearted or just unwilling to start. But you don't have to think in terms of a lifetime.

This forward thinking is what AA calls projection, and it's a killer. Thinking forward to the difficulties that may lie in your future fills your head with fear and hopelessness. So don't do it.

All you have to do is get through today without a drink. Thinking about giving up drink for just one day, the day you are in, is much less frightening. Just concentrate on that. Push tomorrow out of your head and push yesterday out of your head too.

Thinking back will fill your head either with dangerous euphoria or with guilt or with worry. Yesterday is no concern of yours right now; today is the only day that matters. Today is the day you are going to get through without drink.

The ten-minutes-at-a-time plan

Sometimes when the cravings are bad you will probably feel you can't even manage a day – this is the moment you start living not only twenty-four hours at a time but ten minutes at a time.

In the first few days you will probably have times when you feel you are literally going to have to have a drink. The craving is so strong that you feel almost overwhelmed by it.

This is when to live ten minutes at a time. Tell yourself you can get through the next ten minutes or five minutes if necessary without a drink. *Postpone* taking that drink just that long.

You can do it, undoubtedly you can get through ten minutes without having a drink and when that ten minutes is over, start the next ten minutes.

Use the strength of other recovering alcoholics

Before stopping it is wise to make contact with AA. Use the strength of other recovering alcoholics who have done it themselves. They know what you are going through, you don't have to explain; better still, they know how they did it. So listen to what they say, listen to their advice and act on it.

Get to as many meetings as you can. In the first few weeks, if you can fit in two a day – well, do it. If you can only manage one a day then that's fine.

Alcoholics may not share exactly the same experiences with their drinking careers, but their experiences of recovery are more or less identical.

Alcoholics can learn from other recovering people but the most important thing is to get to the meetings. It doesn't matter if you don't follow completely what is going on, it doesn't matter whether you like them or loathe them. Just get your body there, put your bottom on the seat, open your ears and listen.

These meetings are the single most important part of recovering from the illness of alcoholism. Without them you have little chance of remaining sober and happy. With them you have the best chance possible.

If you live in an area where there aren't many meetings you may have to travel miles – but do so. If you haven't got a car use a train or a bus or a taxi. They are expensive but so was your drinking. Getting to meetings is truly worth a fortune.

Besides, you went to any lengths to get a drink. Now go to any lengths to get well.

At first the meetings may seem strange. You will need to go regularly in order to get to know other alcoholics. It's rather like joining a club; you will feel odd and on the outside when you start. At first you won't know anybody, but once you start going regularly you will make friends.

Use that phone

At your first meeting the other people there will offer to give you their phone numbers. Take them. Take every phone number you are offered and use it.

You may feel, 'I shouldn't ring – they're just kind, they don't want to be bothered,' or you may feel embarrassed or awkward about asking for help, your pride may be getting in the way. This is the kind of thinking that interferes with your recovery. People who give you their phone numbers do so in the expectation that you will ring them; you are helping them to remember when they needed help.

And it's the phone that will give you a lifeline at times when you are not at a meeting. You can ring if a craving hits you really hard, you can ring first thing in the morning before you go to work, you can ring when you are frightened of the day, or you can ring last thing at night when you are lying there in the darkness perhaps feeling alone and frightened.

Pick up the phone instead of picking up a drink.

This is an AA saying that has kept many alcoholics clean and sober, but the idea is to pick up the phone *before* the drink, not after.

Staying away from drink

Staying away from the alcohol is really helpful at the beginning. Stay away from your heavy-drinking friends. Stay away from the pub. Maybe even stay away from the street past the pub. Stay away from the road where you bought your drink in the off-licence. Stay away from the cafés and the pubs and the clubs where you used to drink. Stay away from drinking occasions early in your recovery because it is really a set-up to think you can test yourself and still cope.

It's just using common sense and staying away from any situation which may put you at risk until you feel strong enough to handle it.

Stick with the winners

Stay with recovering people who have been sober for a long time. These are the ones who can tell you how they have done it.

Some people in AA are still sick, they are not yet the winners. Some still haven't managed to stop drinking, others have come off so recently they are still confused – these people need help themselves.

Then there are your friends. Well, have a good look at your friends. Are they real friends or are they just drinking pals? 'Of course they are my friends,' you think, but friends or not, they are no good for you at the moment.

Staying around heavy drinkers or other alcoholics should be avoided like the plague in the first few weeks of recovery. For an alcoholic who has just stopped drinking, it isn't helpful to smell alcohol, to be around people who may push drink on you – in other words, to set yourself up.

If you live with a drinker you may even have to consider moving out, at least temporarily; in this instance we are talking about an alcoholic drinker, not a social drinker. It may be helpful to spend some time away from their company, to re-evaluate the relationship.

Putting yourself in a treatment centre is one answer. Very few people indeed manage to stay off drink when their partner is still drinking heavily. Nearly all need to get away for a few days or a few weeks before they can start recovering.

Outside friends or family can be a great help in the first few days if they know what you are attempting to do and if they are trying to understand about alcoholism. They can love you and support you and help you through the first few days.

But some friends just don't understand. It's not that they are alcoholics themselves but just that they don't know the facts of alcoholism. They may try and cheer you up by telling you that you are not really a proper alcoholic. Or they may try and sabotage your efforts. They are not unkind or uncaring, they just don't understand. Avoid them. Later on when you are better and stronger you can get back in touch. You don't need that kind of advice in the first few difficult days or weeks.

Putting your drink problem first

The other secret of staying sober is to make recovery from your drink problem your first priority. Make sure you concentrate all your efforts and your energies on it. For the time being, let the other problems go.

'I can't possibly do that,' you may think, 'my wife has threatened to leave, I'm overdrawn at the bank and my job is at risk. These are all far worse problems – I've got to do something about them. They are more important than stopping drinking.'

This kind of thinking will keep you sick, it really will. Getting off alcohol and staying off is so full of possible setbacks that it simply has to be given priority.

Think it out. If you go on drinking, what's going to happen? Your wife will certainly leave, she's fed up with your drinking anyway. Your finances will undoubtedly get worse and your job will certainly go if you continue to drink – you have probably had warnings about it already.

There isn't a single problem that a drink will make better. It will only make your problems worse.

If, on the other hand, you manage to stay off drink, you stand a far better chance of solving your problems in the long run. You can show your wife that you are sober and that you are changing. You can go to the bank and tell the manager that you are in a mess because of your drinking; then you can work out some kind of plan to put your finances on a safer footing. And you can demonstrate to your boss that you are different and reliable, so your job will no longer be at risk.

All these ways of dealing with the problems depend on your staying sober, so it makes sense to put your drink problem first. Besides, in the first few days of stopping drinking you are simply not well enough to solve any other problems of living. You may feel capable but the truth is that your thinking and your emotions are pretty messed up. For the time being concentrate on not drinking; put the other problems aside for the moment.

Thinking sober

One of the ways to help yourself through the first few days is to do something about your thinking. You may truly want to stop drinking but your mind seems to be full of funny thoughts about continuing to drink. Remember alcoholism is a psychological illness – your mind gets addicted to alcohol too. It may be trying to sabotage your efforts in order to get back to the drink that it craves.

'It was as if my mind was in two parts, the real nice me wanted to stop drinking and get better but the other part wanted to go on drinking. I would have thoughts that perhaps I wasn't really an alcoholic. Or thoughts about drinking again would come into my mind. It's not easy to explain but I had to make sure somehow that I was on the side of the sane part of my mind, the part that wanted to get well. I had to try and replace the drinking with thoughts that helped me to be sober.' That is how one recovering alcoholic put it.

Remembering the bad times

One way to think yourself well is to remember the bad things. They have an expression in AA: 'Remember When'. When thoughts about the good old times come into your head, replace them with thoughts of the bad old times. It is fun when you start drinking but it isn't much fun by the time you stop. The bad things that happen to you can help you get well. Keep them in your mind for the first few days.

One woman who stopped drinking used to recall the Christmas when she was so drunk that she knocked over the Christmas tree, smashed some of the presents and was sick on the carpet. She remembered the look on her children's faces when they told her of that incident early in her recovery. And she wrote the date of that Christmas down and put it on the fridge door so that each morning early in her recovery she remembered that one appalling incident – and she remembered it whenever she felt like a drink.

Another mental trick is to think what will happen if you do drink. Usually when a craving hits you, you think of the first part of drinking, the pleasurable drink, the relief from discomfort. But drinking doesn't end there. You don't stop at one polite glass of sherry; in fact you have probably never had a polite glass of sherry in your life. After the first enjoyable bit comes the 'Well, I handled one, so I can handle more.'

And then there's the excess, the drunkenness, passing out, coming to and the appalling hangovers and the expressions of misery and despair on the faces of your family. And with all these things comes the rest of the drinking behaviour: hurting the ones you say you love, lying, cheating, conning and all the other things that alcoholics do in order to support their drinking behaviour.

All these things follow from the first drink. When a craving hits you and you think about the fun of drinking, think it through past the initial pleasure to the pain you are in now.

Hungry, Angry, Lonely, Tired – HALT

The craving for a drink is likely to hit you in your weak moments. In AA they have evolved a simple acronym, HALT.

If you are hungry, angry, lonely or tired, you are likely to want a drink. So you must avoid being these things by eating properly, by being with supportive people, by getting enough rest.

Anger is a particularly dangerous emotion for recovering people because it turns easily into resentment, and resentment is the habitual way of life for the alcoholic. Therefore you have to try and avoid anger if possible. If you think certain people or situations are likely to fuel your anger, stay away from them or go out of the room rather than have a row.

Of course you are sometimes going to get angry anyway. When that happens, deal with it immediately. Don't sit on it, brood on it, let it simmer and eventually become so uncomfortable that you feel you have to drink. Phone a member of AA or tell a friend. The aim is to get rid of the anger, not to increase it.

Talk it out, dump it. You will be surprised how much you will calm down once you have actually talked about it. If the anger is still there, try physical exercise, go for a swim, enjoy a run, chop wood, dig furiously in your garden, get it out with physical exercise. You will find all these things help. Then talk about it again to other recovering people until it goes away.

The danger in resentment and anger is that it will fester inside you, growing stronger and stronger. There's another AA saying: 'A resentment buried is a resentment buried alive.' Don't go to bed tonight without getting rid of our anger – sitting on it makes it grow. Remember: 'Let not the sun go down on your wrath.'

Be good to yourself

In the first few days you are going to feel confused and ill. You can give yourself some tender loving care such as you would give to somebody you loved who was ill.

Eat some nice food, something that's a favourite of yours. Keep sweets on you – sweet things seem to help those who are trying to get off alcohol. Keep a bar of chocolate in your pocket or your handbag.

Don't try to diet or even to stop smoking when you are first trying to come off alcohol.

Hot, sweet tea makes you feel better and is a good drink when you are first coming off the alcohol. You may not like the sugar but drink it: you need it.

Drink plenty of liquids, just as long as they don't contain alcohol. Make sure there is a variety of soft drinks in your house. Most people feel that they have a craving for sweet things during the withdrawal period. Have fruit juice or cola in the fridge with ice if the weather is hot. Have a variety of drinks so that you won't feel deprived. It is very easy to say, 'Poor me' – and the next phrase is *'Pour me a drink.'*

Finally, pamper your body. Have some hot baths. Buy yourself some new scent. Have your hair done. Do something for yourself that makes you feel better. If you feel clean and smart on the outside it helps you to feel clean on the inside.

Fear and panic

Terrifying fears sometimes hit alcoholics in their first few days of not drinking. Sometimes they are so scared they just go back to the drink.

Occasionally these fears are really indefinable. They seem to come from nowhere and go again. The fear of resuming drinking, however, is not at all bad. Rightly handled it can help you stay off the alcohol. Alcoholics ought to fear the power of drink; a healthy fear will help them stay away.

But sometimes this fear is so intense it seems to be completely demoralising. If you feel that kind of fear, then this is the moment to use the phone and ring AA. If you are without their phone numbers just ring the central office number in Appendix 2.

Many alcoholics describe this paralysing sense of fear – it's not like the fear of something physically terrifying. It is just a terrible sense of impending doom, without anything to tie it on to.

Reading can help. AA will give you certain books to read. Keep one of them by you and just read a bit of it when you get panicky. It really helps. The AA serenity prayer can also help – even if you don't believe in God, because the familiar repetition of these words can deflect your mind from the panic. A prayer, a poem, a slogan – almost anything will do. Repeat it over and again and the repetition will act as a way of calming you.

Hang on in there – no matter what

If you are using the twenty-four-hour plan and the ten-minutes-at-a-time plan for bad moments, you will get through. Sometimes the first few days are full of dreadful moments but just hang on in there. You can do it. Your head may be all over the place, you can't sleep, you can't relax and you are tired all the time. This means you won't cope very well.

You may find that small setbacks, such as missing a bus, put you into a terrible rage. Or when you are stuck in traffic and you feel you are going to scream with the frustration of it all. There may be difficulties at home.

None of these matter in the long run provided you do not use alcohol. Whatever happens, whatever crisis occurs, whatever you do or don't do, in the long run you are doing all right if you are not drinking. Every day is a triumph.

So, don't put yourself down; remember that even if the world seems to be falling apart everything will come all right in the end if you stay away from the drink.

If you are sober you are in there with a good chance, no matter how terrible you feel. If you go back on the bottle, the chance has utterly vanished.

Elation and over-confidence

Sometimes alcoholics feel surges of wild elation in the first few days of not drinking. They may decide that they have beaten the problem, that they don't need any more help, that they can do without AA and their treatment centre.

This absurd over-confidence may lead them to taking risks. They may go back to their drinking friends or their pubs. Their over-confidence may fool them into thinking they can handle these situations. Sooner or later, and it's usually sooner, they go back to drinking.

If you feel this wild confidence, remember that it may be a trick of your mind to get you back into drinking. Suspect your own feelings. Be extra cautious in your recovery.

Make sure you do your recovery the safe way, going to lots of AA meetings, staying away from drinking places or drinkers and trying to do the things that recovering people suggest.

Don't take risks with new-found recovery any more than you would with any other illness. Alcoholism is a subtle, insidious illness. The greatest danger it poses is that of relapse.

Difficulty in stopping

Some people have great difficulty in stopping in their early days of going to AA. They shouldn't despair. If they talk openly to other recovering alcoholics they will probably find somebody else who has had the same problem and who is now happy and sober.

The most important thing is not to lie about your drinking. If you lie to other alcoholics you cut yourself off from the help you need. If you can be honest about the fact that you are still drinking, you will find kindness and help from AA members. Some of them had just as much difficulty stopping.

People who find they cannot stop in AA should go to a specialist treatment clinic or hospital. Sometimes a few weeks away from the habit of drinking helps. Ask recovering people in AA which clinics or hospitals helped them. If this is your problem,

ILLNESS AND RECOVERY*

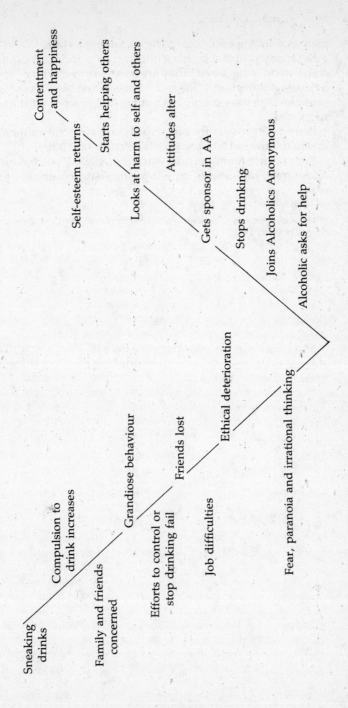

Sneaking drinks

Compulsion to drink increases

Family and friends concerned

Grandiose behaviour

Efforts to control or stop drinking fail

Friends lost

Job difficulties

Ethical deterioration

Fear, paranoia and irrational thinking

Alcoholic asks for help

Joins Alcoholics Anonymous

Stops drinking

Gets sponsor in AA

Attitudes alter

Looks at harm to self and others

Starts helping others

Self-esteem returns

Contentment and happiness

then look in Appendix 2 for help in finding a clinic.

But many people who have difficulty in stopping are not really doing what is suggested. They are not going to meetings, they are not using the phone, they are not sharing their feelings and emotions. They are simply not putting into practice what has been suggested.

Remember, if you are not actually drinking this minute, then you have stopped. *All you have to do is not start again.*

Your twenty-four hours can start from *now*. All you have to do is concentrate your efforts on not taking that first drink – just for today.

* 'Illness and Recovery' diagram reproduced from Max Glatt, *Alcoholism: a Social Disease*, Hodder, 1982.

11

Staying Off Drink

The greatest danger facing recovering alcoholics is that of relapse. Alcoholism is known as the relapsing illness. *Coming off drink is simple: staying off is the real problem.*

That is why no alcoholic should think of himself or herself as cured. As we have said before, the alcoholic is like a diabetic. To stay well a diabetic takes insulin daily but is never cured of the diabetes.

In exactly the same way there is no cure for alcoholism, only a daily recovery – as long as the alcoholic doesn't use alcohol. Once an alcoholic relapses into using drink again, the illness comes back with a vengeance.

Accepting that you cannot drink

To become sober and happy you will have to accept right down in your gut that you cannot drink again nor use mood-altering drugs. This means accepting the fact that even the smallest, tiniest amount of a drink or a drug can bring back the active phase of the illness.

The first sign of relapse usually occurs in the drinker's thinking and the thinking precedes the use of alcohol. It's a myth to say, 'Someone slipped me a drink and I started drinking,' because no one starts drinking like that unless they want to go on drinking. Sometimes relapse occurs because the person fears rejection if he or she doesn't accept a drink or the alcoholic becomes complacent or arrogant and starts to think, 'To hell with it.'

Often the thinking centres around the idea that somehow this time it will be different: this time the alcoholic will be in control, this time he or she will be able to drink like an ordinary social drinker.

It is significant that the AA programme talks of the alcoholic being *powerless* over the addiction. It's not a familiar word to newcomers and you may wonder how it applies to you.

Sometimes when the alcoholic has been sober for a few days subtle thoughts about drinking begin to intrude. 'I can't be an alcoholic because I have stopped,' you may think. This is pretty seductive thinking.

Or the thought will come, 'Well, maybe I can handle just one drink. That won't hurt me.' That alcoholic mind of yours is desperate to think of a reason to drink.

This is where the idea of powerlessness can be helpful. Any alcoholic can give up alcohol altogether. What alcoholics cannot do is constantly control their drinking. For alcoholics it is either abstinence or excess. Moderation is something they cannot handle. It's rather like heavy cigarette smokers – they cannot cut down for any length of time; they have to choose between smoking themselves to death or giving up cigarettes altogether.

One way of seeing how powerless you were over alcohol is to write down ten examples of damage that alcohol did to you. What did it do to your relationships, your finances, your working life, your health and most of all your behaviour?

Now look at those examples. Did you want those things to happen? Of course you didn't. Basically you're not a bad person. You behaved badly because of your drinking. These things happened because you went on drinking and you went on drinking because you had to. Because you were dependent.

That's powerlessness in action and that's why you can't afford even one drink.

The danger of relapse

The thought of using the alcohol comes first, the actual using follows. Just one drink and it will all come back. It will activate further the irrational thinking that leads inevitably back to the heavy drinking. Once again it starts eating away in your head.

The emotional disorder will come right back and the crazy thinking will start again.

And it won't stop there. You will relapse back into the illness's active phase and may suffer again for years. You cannot count on being able to stop again. Any long-standing AA member can tell of tragic alcoholic relapses and the consequential funerals they have attended. You may well have another drink in you, but you may not have another recovery.

It doesn't matter how long you have been sober. The illness is lying dormant within you and it can be activated after twenty years of sober living by just one drink.

Alas, you don't start from the beginning when you resume your drinking. Many times it starts at the point at which you left off. It may even be worse after that length of time as if it has progressed while it lay dormant.

Bill

Bill was an alcoholic who had been sober and happy for fifteen years. He started to talk about himself as cured. He started to show off about his recovery to his friends. His friends warned him about this kind of thinking but Bill wouldn't listen. He became arrogant and grandiose, and it wasn't long before he was telling himself that he could now handle *a* drink.

Within a month he was drinking a bottle *a day*. His wife and children were shattered and Bill's pride was such that he couldn't contemplate getting help again.

Within three months Bill was dead. And he wasn't even fifty.

You don't have to accept what we say on trust. You can see for yourself by going to AA and watching other people. They will demonstrate the truth of this. You will see what happens if people relapse. They don't come back to AA boasting of the good time they had. If they manage to make it back at all, they will tell stories of how this time it was worse than ever.

If you don't believe this and you want to test it out here and now, ask around in the next AA meeting for somebody who has had a relapse and they will tell you themselves what happened. Luckily you don't have to learn this sadness by personal experience. You can let others demonstrate it for you and you can learn from their experience.

Make yourself aware of the dangers of relapse. Once you have seen it demonstrated in front of your eyes you will know why you must put effort not just into stopping but into staying stopped.

How to cope socially early in recovery

Some people feel awkward or embarrassed at their first social occasion in recovery. Let's face it, they have probably never been out socially in their adult life without a drink.

The first time you go to a social occasion the best way to cope is just to accept that it is *your* body, *your* mind; it is for *you* to decide what you want to drink.

When your host asks you what you would like to drink, don't say, 'I don't drink.' Just say, 'I would like a Perrier, or an orange juice or a ginger ale.'

Make a positive request and you will find it is no big deal. If a drink is pushed on you just say, 'I don't drink.' You don't have to justify it and you will find that after a while the people who want to drink are more interested in their own drinking and really don't give a damn what you drink.

Altering attitudes

If you want to stay sober you will eventually find that you have to change the way you live, because the lifestyle of the drinking alcoholic is no good for the recovering alcoholic. One of the secrets of staying stopped is to alter your attitudes.

AA members often say that the initials of their fellowship stand, not just for Alcoholics Anonymous, but for Altered Attitudes. If you think about it you will see that this is sensible. In fact, if you are successfully staying off drink you are probably already practising it.

For example you are probably already changing the way you think about drink. Instead of thinking about the pleasures of drinking you are thinking about the pain it has caused you and others. You have 'altered your attitude' towards drink and that new attitude is helping you stay away from it.

But this is just a beginning. There are many other attitudes which in the long run need changing.

Drinking has affected your life and the way you think and feel in many ways. You may not yet know the full extent of what your alcoholism has done to you. For many years psychologists, doctors and psychiatrists have been studying alcoholics. They have come to the conclusion that dependence on alcohol is not just a physical illness – it is also an emotional illness and there are a group of characteristics that most alcoholics have that we have already described in Chapter 3, characteristics such as arrogance, over-sensitivity, self-pity, an inability to stand frustration and anger, an unwillingness to face reality, fear and dishonesty.

Healthier personality traits

For the alcoholic to get well, these characteristics need to be replaced by healthier personality traits:

– the arrogance must be replaced with humility;
– over-sensitivity with care for other people's needs;
– self-pity with gratitude;
– inability to stand frustration with patience and emotional control;
– anger with tolerance and caring;
– inability to face reality with acceptance of what reality really is;
– fear with trust;
– dishonesty with honesty.

You may feel that some of these words are rather a turn-off. Words like 'humility' for instance sound rather like something out of Sunday school.

Don't let these feelings blind you to what we are saying. Take humility, for example. We don't suggest you become a grovelling Uriah Heep. A person who is humble is just somebody who is able to see that he or she is not perfect and is able to admit mistakes. Therefore the humble person is able to learn. Put like this there isn't anything wrong with humility; it's a question of adapting to the reality of what you are actually like.

But how on earth is the alcoholic – just off alcohol, confused and probably feeling awful – going to do all this? How can an alcoholic a few days away from a drink start changing?

The Twelve Steps

This is where AA will help you. AA has a recovery programme of Twelve Steps, or stages to recovery (see Appendix 1). These have been worked out from the experience of recovering alcoholics in the past half-century.

By following these steps they discovered they were able to stay away from drink, not just now and then, for the odd day or two, but for years. And, better still, by practising these steps they discovered how to be happy without drink.

For the aim of the Twelve Steps is nothing less than happiness. After all, to be sober does not mean holding on by the skin of your teeth. Continuing unhappiness will only lead you to wonder if it wouldn't be better to have another drink.

As we said before, alcoholics are not bad people trying to be good. They are sick people trying to get well, and the Twelve Steps of AA are the method by which hundreds and thousands of alcoholics have recovered their emotional health and their personal dignity.

They were originally written down as a factual record of how the first hundred alcoholics from AA recovered.

Many people coming to AA for the first time today, however, sometimes find them a little too religious to accept. And so we would like to offer an interpretation of the Twelve Steps which keeps to their original spirit but makes them more accessible to newcomers.

We believe that the steps are a vital part of recovery for alcoholics:

1. Admit to your problem and to its effect on your life.

2. Believe that AA can help you get better.

3. Be willing to do what AA suggests.

4. Get honest with yourself about the things you did when you used alcohol.

5. Get honest with somebody else about it – usually your AA sponsor.

6. Readily admit that faulty attitudes need changing.

7. Be ready to co-operate with AA in changing your attitudes.

8. List the harm caused to others by your drinking.

9. Try to put that right, where possible.

10. Get into the habit of being honest with yourself and admitting mistakes.

11. Be willing to accept that you are not the centre of the universe and that there are greater forces in the world.

12. Help other alcoholics recover and lead a new and healthy life with better values.

Because the Twelve Steps benefit alcoholics it is important they should be put into practice. You don't have to do them all today.

They are numbered in order. Start with number 1 and then gradually work your way through them. There are no deadlines: recovery is a developing process, not an event. Most people spend weeks on the first step and sometimes months before starting on the others.

And the best way to do them is to find a friend to guide you through them. That friend will normally be your AA sponsor.

Getting a sponsor

When you have been in AA meetings for a number of weeks, regularly, you start getting to know the other people there. Just like any group of people you will find some that you like and others that you are less keen on.

Newcomers need a sponsor if they are to make progress towards recovery. The point of this is to find a friend who has done it before and who can therefore give you the benefit of his or her support, comfort and experience.

Find somebody who has been in AA for at least two years and who has been completely sober during that period. A member who has had periods back on drink is somebody who is clearly having difficulty with the programme. For a sponsor you need someone who has been practising the programme successfully.

It is better really to have a sponsor of the same sex. The idea is to avoid having emotional or sexual entanglements. If the relationship works you will find yourself getting very close to your sponsor, which could lead to complications or a love affair if you are not of the same sex.

Of course, gay men and women may want to have sponsors of the opposite sex in order to avoid this possibility. The guiding principle is to choose a sponsor who will be a friend, not a lover.

Choose somebody that you trust and like. It's no good having a sponsor whom you don't care for, since this will make it much more difficult to confide in them. Sometimes people choose sponsors from a similar background to themselves, other times they choose sponsors who are quite different. It doesn't matter as long as you trust them and it works for you.

The greatest advantage in a sponsor is having somebody who knows all about you. It's like a good, long-term friend who can talk out the difficulties with you and will know enough about you to know what is going on in your life.

At the beginning of your membership of AA you may not know enough people to be sure who you want as a sponsor, but you can always ask somebody to act in a temporary capacity until you make your choice.

In the first few months of being sober lots of painful emotions surface. Living without alcohol is not always easy and sometimes life seems full of anxious moments or difficulties. Having a friend to confide these things to makes it much easier to bear.

A sponsor is there to be *used*. Ideally it should be someone you see reasonably regularly in the course of your meetings. Regular phone contact is also very important. A sponsor you neither see nor telephone cannot help you, and of course *it is up to you to ask for the help.*

Getting involved in AA

Newly recovering alcoholics need a routine of AA meetings, where they can see people they know and where they can start to feel comfortable. This not only makes for friendship but also acts as a kind of check on the mental side of recovery.

People who have been sober for a long time and get to know you will notice if you are going through a bad time or showing signs of dangerous thinking that may lead back to a drink – and they can help you.

Just going to meetings is probably all you can manage in the first few days and weeks of recovery but as you begin to feel calmer and more sober you will need to do a little bit more to get the full benefit of recovery within AA. Getting involved by doing some of the small tasks around the meetings will help you recover.

One of the most important things for an alcoholic is to begin to change from a life of self-obsession towards a life of helping others.

'Several months after I started going to AA somebody asked me if I would do the teas, which involved buying the milk on the way to the meeting. I was terrified at first,' recalls Ben. 'Although I was in my fifties I still found it very difficult to talk to strangers. I felt very shy but as I had been asked I thought I had better do it. So I started getting the milk and I started doing the teas and after a while found myself almost looking forward to it.

'It was an easy way to start talking to people. As I handed out the tea or the coffee, I began to feel in a small way that I was doing something worthwhile. It was a small beginning but it made all the difference to my recovery.'

Difficulties with AA

Some people take to AA without any trouble at all. As soon as they walk in they have a feeling, which they describe later, of coming home. They are immediately able to accept the friendship offered and are quite happy to do what is suggested.

For some, however, the opposite occurs, and if you are one of those people who don't like the meetings at first, try to think of them as a treatment for your illness. For instance, if you had cancer you would accept the radium treatment, for even if such treatment is uncomfortable or even painful you know that it will help you to recover.

It may help you to think of AA in this way even if for the time being you don't enjoy it. But that is not the point. Like medicine it is good for you whether you enjoy it or not. So keep going and after a while you will begin to see the sense of it all.

It will help if you go to several different meetings. Their exact format varies. Some are large with lots of people; others are quite small and intimate. Some have speakers, some are discussions, some talk about the Twelve Steps of the AA programme. Going around several meetings allows you to find one at which you feel at home.

Many newcomers in AA are upset when they hear people talking about God – it makes them feel very uncomfortable and embarrassed. But begin to think of the difference between spirituality and organised religion.

Sometimes believers are just as horrified as unbelievers, yet if they just keep going they will discover that the membership includes many people like them who were initially worried by the idea of God.

A belief in God is not necessary to belong to AA. People with no faith can recover in the Twelve-Step programme just as well as believers. What is important is to get out of the driver's seat, stop doing it your way – in other words, stop playing God.

A spiritual not a religious programme

It is important to realise that the programme of recovery is not a religious one. You do not have to have any religious belief in order to practice it.

But it is a spiritual programme. It is designed to help your spirit, the inner you, to recover from the harm alcoholism has done to you. Chemical dependence is a threefold illness: it harms the body, the mind and the spirit of the alcoholic.

Exactly how you interpret spirituality is up to you. Some people think of it as what concerns the ethical part of the human being. Others think of it as the soul. Some people think of it as the conscience. Still others are happy with the idea of an inward spirit. Others are religious according to their traditions. You are free to interpret things as you choose in AA.

But taking care of the spiritual takes care of the feelings of loneliness, self-disgust and self-loathing that have been with you for such a long time.

In the same way, you can give the word God whatever meaning you choose. Some people try and think of it as just the good in themselves and others. Others concentrate on the idea that they cannot recover from alcoholism on their own and so they need a higher power of some kind. This higher power can be the power of the group, stronger than any individual strength, or the philosophy of AA, or the Twelve Steps of recovery. Once again you are free to choose whatever makes sense to you.

Those with a lot of intellectual pride sometimes find this difficult. They are so used to using their brains to solve their problems that they tend to think themselves out of AA. This keeps them very sick. If you are plagued with intellectual doubts, use your brain to think yourself into AA. That way you will get well.

Doing it your way is doing it the wrong way

Some alcoholics have an overwhelming confidence that their way of getting sober is better than anyone else's. They may be unwilling to follow the suggestions of AA or unwilling even to consider them. They still want to do things 'their way'.

This problem of unwillingness afflicts many alcoholics just off the drink. It is part of the way the sick mind tries to make excuses to go back to drinking.

This is where will power can help you get well. If you feel unwilling to do the things suggested you use your will power to do them, even if you don't want to. *Make* yourself go to a meeting, however much they make you feel uncomfortable. *Make* yourself listen and at least consider the ideas put to you.

The truth is you are 99 per cent likely to be wrong. Alcoholics who are still drinking have their minds and hearts distorted by the drug of alcohol. A drinking alcoholic cannot think clearly. They do not know better than those who have been sober for months and years.

Look at it like this. For years you have been doing it your way. But what was your way? It was a lifestyle that involved drinking, and drinking became the be-all and end-all. Doing it your way made you ill and kept you ill.

Do you really want it that way? For if you do things your way, you will go back to drinking.

You don't have to do it all at once

If you are one of the unwilling ones, concentrate on getting to meetings, getting involved, and getting a sponsor. Regular attendance at meetings, keeping clear of alcohol and alcoholic situations are essentials. Practise doing the little things people suggest, because many of the small practical suggestions of how to stay away from alcohol and how to deal with drinking situations are easy to accept.

You will notice that alcoholics in recovery often do not give advice directly. Instead they talk about what they did and how the programme worked for them. Is it possible to take offence at this? After all they are only relating their own experience of recovery.

Their experience can help you if you let it. Of course, everyone is different and what works for one may not work for others. For example, the experience of someone with a marital problem may not be the same as yours nor provide any help for you, but at least you know somebody else had the problem and was able to deal with it.

When people have the same kind of trouble, the experience of long-standing members of AA can usually help you. Somebody who has been going through strain in a marriage can help you as you go through the strain of yours in the first few weeks in recovery, when your family don't really believe that anything is going to be different.

Trust in AA

Getting sober is like a leap in the dark. You are bound to be worried and frightened about the future. You are at the beginning of an enormous change in your life. In the first few weeks you may have a lot of doubts and fears.

Trust in AA. Of course the future seems scary but when so many alcoholics around you are staying sober thanks to doing what the programme says, it is overwhelmingly likely that it will work for you too. Remind yourself of all the happy alcoholics who used to feel just as down, just as miserable, just as frightened, just as angry as you, but who are now making it. All you have to do is do it today.

Unwillingness can and does change to willingness just as long as you stay close to AA. As long as you stay away from drink and keep going to the meetings you will recover.

12

Women Alcoholics: Their Special Problems and How to Treat Them

For all the cries of equality, if you are a woman with a drinking problem you are quite likely to be looked upon with distaste, if not contempt. If a man drinks too much and makes a fool of himself, everyone laughs and probably thinks he is a hell of a guy, as he carouses, breaks up pubs and has a succession of women. As a woman you are seen either as an easy lay or as a loser.

Men seem to drink longer and in a more damaging way than women, and are tolerated for far longer. Luckily or unluckily, alcoholism seems to catch up with a woman very fast. This is a fact of life and there is no point in pretending it does not exist.

It is even usual for fathers to take their sons to a pub as a sign of coming of age. It is still seen as *macho*, even laudable, to be able to 'hold your drink like a man'. Can you imagine the scenario of Mum taking daughter to the pub to introduce her to the girls and encouraging her to drink?

Women are not so easily accepted as alcoholics

Ten years ago in our treatment unit there were about four men to every one woman. Now it is about half and half with women perhaps tending to predominate.

It is irrelevant whether alcoholism in women is actually on the increase or whether it is simply being diagnosed more often. What is important is to understand the special problems of women alcoholics.

This is a chapter specifically addressed to women. However, we are not of course saying that only women feel guilt and remorse or have the prerogative in pain. Far from it. Men have exactly the same feelings and emotions, and likewise suffer from guilt and remorse. In fact women have to be careful that they do not dismiss men's feelings and play the helpless little woman. But women are usually not so easily accepted as alcoholic and this is why their problems need to be specially highlighted.

Physical deterioration

Women seem to go out of control with their drinking at a younger age than men. The physical damage often takes over faster. A woman's looks deteriorate rapidly with alcoholic drinking: her hair becomes dry and lifeless, her face becomes puffy and her skin gets that crêpey look. Lines and wrinkles seem to show more and this is all quite apart from the physical damage described in Chapter 3.

Emotional damage

But the most damaging effect for women takes place in the realm of feeling. Alcoholics are on the whole people with very high standards and a sensitive conscience. This may surprise you as their behaviour is so often just the opposite.

When they drink, they experience terrible guilt and remorse, as well as an appalling sense of shame that is often nearly unbearable. This is, of course, great fuel for continued drinking. Alcoholics drink, behave badly, loathe themselves and then drink again. They drink to find oblivion from their painful feelings. Then this senseless, destructive circle starts all over again.

Why? It is fairly pointless wracking one's brains, because nobody really knows the answer. There are masses of theories: I drink because I am afraid, because I am alone, because my boyfriend left me, because Daddy gave me too much as a child, because I am deprived, because my children left home and I am not needed any more.

Actually, you drink because you have an illness called alcoholism, where your drinking is slowly but progressively going out of control. *The drink is using you rather than you using a drink.*

It doesn't matter whether you are sixteen or sixty, you can be an alcoholic. Some will start pinching booze from their parents at thirteen or fourteen and are on nearly a bottle of spirits a day by the time they are twenty. You could still be holding down a job and no one even knows about your alcoholism, or you might be at college and getting by somehow.

Some women take five to fifteen years to get really into trouble. It doesn't matter whether you are a housewife or a solicitor. You can be an alcoholic and you can recover.

Ann's story

'When I left my home town in Canada, aged twenty, to study abroad for a year,' recalls Anne, 'I carried in my suitcase a few samples of a so-called "appetite-suppressant", supplied by my kindly family physician, who knew I was forever struggling to shed a few pounds. On the ship to France I discovered mixed drinks, and thus began my long love-affair with mood-altering chemicals, which up until then I had felt no desire or need for. The twenty-year merry-go-round of uppers and downers, losing and gaining weight, speeding up and slowing down, excesses in everything from sleep to athletics, had begun in earnest.

'My tolerance for alcohol, and later on for tranquillisers, was fairly high, and apart from two or three occasions during the early years of my marriage when I was falling down drunk, the disease of alcoholism was not apparent to the "layman", not even to one as close to me as my husband.

'After the birth of our second child when I was twenty-nine, I was consuming by myself half a bottle of wine by the early evening and my frequent aggressiveness led my husband to believe I was falling out of love with him.

'His guilt and puzzlement grew until he found a book, "Recovery from Alcoholism", three years later in 1975, by which point I had begun "secretly" buying and hiding my bottles, passing out in odd places such as the laundryroom or the bathroom floor, and suffering my first memory-lapses or blackouts. We both experienced embarrassment over my "forgotten" appointments and telephone conversations, but I refused to discuss the relevance of what my husband discovered in that book to what was happening to me.

'It was not for another three years, during which time my

periodic bouts of drunkenness and related personality changes escalated in their frequency and seriousness, that a friend introduced my husband to Al-anon and explained to him that alcoholism was a disease, not a moral weakness or fault. But I continued to deny any problem whatsoever, all the while pretending to be abstinent just to keep the peace and at the same time increasing my consumption on the sly. It took another of my drunken, nasty outbursts to finally open his eyes.

'After my first hospitalisation in 1979 for what I called "blood-tests", but what was really a detoxification, my husband had me agree in front of a lawyer to "do something" about my drinking or be faced with divorce proceedings.

'I thus began attending AA meetings and swallowing Antabuse tablets to keep my side of the bargain; but I just mouthed the words "I am an alcoholic" and played games with the tablets and the drinks, remaining less than convinced that I really was an alcoholic.

'Meanwhile my children were growing up, suffering the embarrassment and fear of a giggling, glassy-eyed mother who tried too hard to be a "pal" to their friends, and who was drunk behind the wheel of the car more and more frequently.

'The next stage was a treatment centre in Canada, which at my husband's insistence I attended as an out-patient for a month, staying with my mother, who had always been very supportive of me but was of course terrified when she witnessed my extreme personality changes and mood swings.

'I learned a great deal, medically speaking, about the disease of alcoholism, and felt very sorry for the nine men in my group, who were all sick, lonely, unemployed and/or divorced.

'I still could not understand, or accept, how I, a healthy, optimistic, athletic extrovert, lucky and happy with my husband and two children, could possibly be an alcoholic: I didn't have a "reason" to drink the way the others did! I had not yet accepted alcoholism as a disease that strikes mankind indiscriminately.

'After treatment I did not drink for eight months, but took the occasional sleeping-pill, not mentioning it of course at AA meetings. I rarely talked about feeling angry or upset, and when I did pick up the first drink, I called my sponsor afterwards.

The binge-abstention merry-go-round began in earnest in early 1980, and I made a suicide attempt with pills, leaving a note telling the family they would be better off with me dead. I got drunk again after being released from hospital. My husband had begun telling me to leave the house when I started a binge, and after the overdose the forced separation lasted four weeks.

'I didn't drink, but attended AA every day, started to pray for help, and used the telephone constantly. I kept busy with my volunteer teaching job, and I played tennis and squash. I felt dreadfully sorry for myself at being excluded from my daughter's 12th birthday celebration until an AA friend rightly told me she was far better off without me than having me there drunk on the floor.

'I returned home joyously repentant and abstinent on St Valentine's Day.

'A calm period ensued; the family developed a little trust in me; I suffered three bouts of illness without resorting to bottle or pill and the honeymoon lasted four months, until I drank some wine I had kept after a party. During this, my worst binge to date, and after I had been away from home for ten days, my husband gave me an ultimatum I believed he would stick to: a treatment centre in England which I had heard from fellow AA members was very tough, or divorce. He could stand no more, and feared for his own and our children's health.

'Thus began the eight weeks that saved my life; the eight weeks that I look back on as my life's most important experience. I was forced to look at myself and listen to how the others perceived me. I had to face criticism and confrontation and then *express* my anger and frustration, not smile sweetly as I had always done, being a born "people-pleaser". I had to start to accept that I could *not* be tops at everything or the most popular person around. Self-acceptance was the bottom line.

'It was tough to come home two months later to my loved ones who had managed very well without me, and who were of course sceptical about my recovery.

'For the next seven months I really enjoyed AA meetings. I talked about my feelings, negative and positive, and was much more open about any disagreement I felt. I was less of a "people-pleaser", and more confident about my own opinions.

'I had to drink again, however, perhaps to prove to myself that alcoholism really is incurable.

'My fear and desperation were far more intense during this final binge, and I jumped at the chance to go into treatment again for a week to really look at what emotions I had been repressing: jealousy and resentment, all stemming from my overwhelming pride about what people think of me. I still had a long way to go towards self-acceptance (and the voyage will never be over!).

'Of course I had once again broken down my family's sense of security and confidence, but over the past four and a half years of my sobriety we have worked together on our "life's programme", doing our best to discuss openly how we feel about each other and about personal relations.

'I have had to accept many "consequences" of my years of crazy behaviour, but today I firmly believe that my two teenagers have a certain head-start, on their road to maturity, from having known shame and suffering, from having witnessed my recovery from addiction, and from having become aware of the dangers of obsessive behaviour and the importance of expressing feelings. My marriage as a result is now one of a deeper sense of togetherness, understanding and mutual appreciation than it probably would have been had we enjoyed plain sailing all the way.

'I can only thank God and the AA fellowship for my great good fortune in having had a wonderful husband who stood by me but confronted me when necessary, and in having enjoyed good health despite years of bodily abuse. I am also lucky that I took the push towards recovery early enough so that I can still enjoy my children's development and friendship. Day by day, life gets better and better in recovery,and what is perhaps most important, I now enjoy being the person who is me.'

As you can see, Ann was loved, she had a good marriage and two children and she was in most people's terms comfortably off materially. But she also had acquired the illness of alcoholism. And yet, she has recovered from it.

The distortion of a whole lifestyle

Many women start drinking at home as housewives with a couple of children. Your drinking may begin when you go out with your husband. You might notice that you are shy or nervous and that if you have a couple of drinks you feel better.

Then you may start to have one before you go out to release you from that tension. At a party or a dance you start to get restless if the drinks come too slowly, or are bored until you reach a certain level of alcohol in your system.

For many years this may not show as a problem, and then you may find yourself picking up that extra bottle at the supermarket and telling yourself you *may* have friends in at the weekend. They don't come but you have a few drinks anyway, and it seems fairly normal. You like the sensation, it makes you feel good.

After a while you tell yourself, 'Goodness, I have had a tough morning. I will have a glass of wine with my lunch – or two.'

It is now that it starts getting sneaky and catching up with you.

Before long half a bottle has gone at lunchtime every day.

Your husband comments that you seem to be drinking a lot. He can't keep up. You snap his head off and tell him to mind his own business.

Most of your afternoons are spent having a nap. The children come in and you are edgy and irritable. They are full of their day but all you want is another drink. They soon learn to keep out of your way. They are bewildered and confused and don't know what they have done wrong.

You start avoiding social events and family gatherings because you can't then drink the way you want to.

You start being glad if your husband is out because then you can drink what you want with no comment, but you also scream at him if he is out a lot. Both are nice excuses to have another drink.

Before long there are bad vibes and terrible fights most of the time around the house and people start walking around you on eggshells. Your husband stays out even more as he can't stand what he finds when he comes home, and this to your drinking mind justifies your behaviour.

By now the drink is damaging your health, your family, and most of all yourself. You are sick of your lying, sneaky behaviour, the self-disgust at hiding bottles around the house, the sense of shame of going to endless different off-licences, never going to the same one twice in a week as you think somehow, someone will catch you out.

No wonder women suffer so terribly from shame. A whole lifestyle is distorted with drinking.

Passivity and anger

One of the most destructive aspects in women who drink is their passivity. Traditionally women have been taught to be relatively passive creatures, feminine, accepting, looking to Dad or their husbands for financial, material and emotional support. Many alcoholic women feel that someone should always look after them.

This doesn't mean that alcoholic women are weak or pathetic – far from it. They are usually bright, sensitive and very determined when it comes to having their own way, but they have found that it pays to play helpless, to be the victim all the time. It is so easy to blame others when life isn't exactly the way you want. Then you don't have to take any responsibility for your own behaviour.

Many women that we see in our clinic initially come over as nice, well-mannered women. Push a little and there is a reservoir of rage that is truly frightening. Anger with parents, anger with the children, anger with their husband – usually it is the husband – who have left in despair or who out of desperation have become very controlling in their behaviour.

But the alcoholic woman seldom deals with these negative feelings: she just drinks on them. The fear of asserting herself is awesome. It's safer to be passive and angry and drink on it, than to change the way she is to what she could be.

Losing your husband

Many women have lost their husbands or their partners because of their drinking and the behaviour that follows. Men are more inclined to leave an alcoholic woman than vice versa. The main reason for this is financial and material. More men than women have jobs and careers so it is easier for them to support themselves and their children.

For the alcoholic woman this is just another excuse to drink – 'My husband left me for another woman. No wonder I drink' is the usual statement. 'My husband is a workaholic, he is never at home.' She never stops to think that she wasn't very nice and attractive to come home to.

If you take a careful history you will find that in the majority of cases the drinking long predates the problem. The alcoholic woman just uses these excuses as a peg on which to hang her drinking. Because of the sense of hopelessness, anger, despair and shame, women are more likely to look for 'reasons' for their drinking, whereas most men just say they enjoyed it, at least in the beginning!

If you are an alcoholic woman and you want to recover, you must accept that you have a problem with alcohol and you must do the following:

1. *You must stop drinking.* You can never return to the odd sherry or glass of wine because it will always escalate.

2. *You must stop wallowing in self-pity and vain regret.* You can't change one iota of the past but you can change the present and the future.

3. *You must recognise and change the anger and resentment that made you a bitter and hateful person.* Resentment means getting less from someone when you expected more. Ask yourself whether your

expectations were reasonable. Was it reasonable to expect your husband to put up forever with your unattractiveness, your unlovingness, your bad moods every time he came home? Could you really expect him to do all the shopping and cooking, look after the children, be nice and reasonable and loving? Isn't this too much to expect? Did you also expect him to make love to you when you stank of booze and stale sweat? Ask yourself.

4. *You must stop judging yourself.* You are sick, not bad, and if you are sick you can be well. You don't have to hold on to the shame and guilt that you feel and use it as yet another excuse to drink. You are not the worst person in the world, even if you feel it. You may have been a bitch, you may have slept around, you may have screamed at the children and been rude to your friends. But you did those things because you drank. You don't drink because of these things. So stop drinking and change.

Harriet's story: a happy and successful recovery

Harriet changed. Today she is married, has a career in the media and is a happy, successful woman.

'I stopped drinking', she says, 'when it started to hurt. I got so drunk I couldn't put the key in the door. In fact we have just had the door decorated so you can't see the scratches any more!

'I drank to the point that I couldn't remember. I drank and woke up in bed with someone whose name I had to ask. I drank and became aggressive and rude at dinner parties and had to write notes to apologise for the behaviour I only dimly remembered.

'It came to the point where I had a constant feeling of impending madness and most of the time felt completely paranoid. I was sure that people were talking about me but at the same time at the back of my head I knew they were not.

'I asked for a leave of absence to get myself together but it didn't work. I became very frightened. I changed my job but that didn't work either.

'One morning I woke up in bed with my husband and said, "Thank God it's you." At this point I called AA. I had been avoiding this because I knew they would require me to stop drinking.

'I went and for the first few weeks I was asking myself who are these nuts? They are so much worse than me, I am not that bad. But they made sense.

'I thought maybe I could learn to drink like normal people but then I realised – I'm not interested in two polite sherries – what's the point? In fact it still makes me giggle seeing normal drinkers drink.

'I met one man in AA who was a lot older and very successful, and not my idea of a drunk at all. He helped me and made me see that recovery was possible.

'I also got a woman sponsor who had been sober for a long time.

'To these two people I probably owe my life and my peace of mind. I felt a lot of guilt and shame over my drinking behaviour. Talking it through with them I could let go of it.

'I also heard others in the meetings who had behaved the same way as me because of their drinking, and this was such a release. I had always thought that I was the only one.

'At first in AA I just sat and listened, and after a while I got a bit fed up. I started questioning – do I need this? I was told to get involved, even if it was only helping collect up the dirty ashtrays and make the tea. Talk to the newcomers, don't be so self-centred. This really helped, I started to feel something and to care for other people.

'I started really looking at the AA programme and its Twelve Steps. I worked at them myself rather than just paying lip-service to them, and it all started to fall into place.

'I work in a profession that is surrounded by drunks and I wanted to stay in my career and lead a normal life, not be a hermit and isolate myself just because I had an illness called alcoholism. I can do this today surrounded more than most by drinkers and drinking. If I go regularly to AA it works.

'I can't change others in my life but I can change *me*. I had to change my attitudes and keep them changed. I had to accept that others can drink. I used to feel that this was very unfair. When I said this I was told, "Don't be so childish. You have a nice house, a loving husband and a good job. It's pathetic not to expect some difficulties in your life."

'Get to know people in AA. Don't stay on your own and creep out before the end of the meeting. Stay and talk to people. I probably wouldn't be alive today if I hadn't gone to AA. Go regularly, make friends, practise the Twelve Steps of recovery. Get to like yourself and others, rather than hating yourself and criticising everyone else.

'The choice to drink has gone. You have a choice to change and become a different and happier person.

'Life for me now is great, despite the problems that everyone has. Happy and fun. A full life, a hectic social life, a good marriage and a satisfying career. I am not a crippled human being as once I thought I was.

'Stick with AA. You will find lots of love, lots of caring, and it gives you the energy to get on with your recovery. AA is fun and there is often a lot of laughter as you get more and more involved. Just try it, it works.'

PART FIVE

Recovery

13

A Healthy Body

Alcohol can damage the body as well as the mind and the emotions, but physically most alcoholics recover very quickly, even when their alcoholism has been severe. Older alcoholics may face a longer period of physical recovery but for most people it's a great idea to get back to normal living as soon as possible. An active and happy life is far better protection against relapse than just sitting around feeling sorry for yourself.

Taking care of your body by getting proper food, rest and relaxation is part of recovery. So eat proper meals, plenty of fresh fruit and vegetables. Give yourself enough rest. The mind and the body are connected. If your body is unwell it will translate that feeling of unwellness to your mind and you will probably start feeling low and anxious.

It's rather like running a car. If you have never serviced or maintained it, it is going to break down. In the same way you wouldn't expect a car to run from London to Edinburgh without filling up with petrol. In exactly the same way you need to look after your body and your mind.

Exercise and relaxation

Many alcoholics have difficulty in relaxing in the first few months of recovery. For years they have been sedated with alcohol and when that is no longer available they find it difficult to relax naturally. People who have used tranquillisers, or who have been cross-dependent on tranquillisers and alcohol, particularly suffer from this inability to unwind. Exercise is probably the best natural way of helping to relax. A body that is physically tired relaxes naturally and sleep often comes better at the end of the day.

But be sensible. Alcoholics need to take extra care not to overdo things; start slowly and move on gently so that you don't overstrain yourself.

Sometimes for people who find it particularly hard it's worthwhile getting some relaxation tapes or even going to some relaxation classes. You will find some helpful addresses in Appendix 3.

Women and health

Women have particular problems in recovery. Sometimes their bodies don't function the way they should. Sometimes women have trouble with their periods; they have missed them or not had them while they were drinking. They may take a while to return to normal. Perhaps period pains start to bother them for the first time for years because they are not anaesthetised by drink. After years of living under sedation it can be quite a surprise to feel ordinary pain. Alcoholics in the early stages of recovery are bad at enduring pain or discomfort. Make sure that you watch out for this – don't reach for the pills and start getting in on that route to dependence.

Relaxation is a great way to deal with period pains. Make yourself lie down and relax; also do some physical exercise. That really does get rid of the pain, if you concentrate on it.

Drinking and sex

Sex is often a problem with recovering people because they may have never entered into an intimate or sexual relationship without drink. When you first sober up, you start to feel very awkward and uncomfortable in this area. Yet drink, as the drunk porter in *Macbeth* said 'provokes desire but it takes away the performance.'

Many alcoholics have lived very distorted sex lives under the influence of alcohol and have behaved in ways they very much regret when sober. When you sober up it usually takes some little time for this side of life to settle down. Time is needed to heal the emotional wounds and to sort out your sexual life.

'Drinking was always associated with sex, and I always had rather unsatisfactory and rather sordid relationships and it seemed to me that sex is another appetite like booze,' says a recovering alcoholic.

In addition drink distorts sexual behaviour. Some women are sexually abused while under the influence of drink, others become sexually promiscuous. Some women alcoholics become prostitutes and some male alcoholics, including those who are heterosexual, enter into homosexual relationships, which they wouldn't think of doing if they were sober. This sometimes leads to sexual infections and becomes in turn just another cause of the self-loathing and self-disgust which can be part of a drink lifestyle.

There is an awful lot of drink and remorse in most alcoholics who have been involved in sexual behaviour which contravenes their own standards of behaviour. This needs attending to as you get into recovery, perhaps by talking it through with your sponsor.

Another problem is a fear of intimacy, a fear of letting anyone get close to you. The fear of being vulnerable is so great that many alcoholics have to re-learn the gift of intimacy as their recovery progresses.

Getting rid of the past

In AA there is a way to deal with the sexual guilt of the past. AA suggests making a kind of inventory of destructive behaviour and then talking it over with a trusted person: your sponsor, a minister or priest, or if you are in treatment your therapist. This is what is called taking the fourth and fifth steps in the AA programme of recovery. This obviously doesn't just apply to sexual problems, but to any areas where you feel guilt, shame or remorse.

The advantage of following this advice is that it helps to draw the line under the past. Often the temptation is just to put the past under the carpet. This does not work. Dealing with the feelings is the only way. Bring them out into the daylight. Talk about them and then dump them.

The way to emotional recovery is to face and accept the pain of the past and then to put it behind you. It takes enormous courage to do this but it is a vital part of getting well. Guilt and anxiety fade away through putting the fourth and fifth steps into action.

It is not usually a good idea, however, to confess everything to your partner. You will just be unloading your own guilt at the expense of their peace of mind.

In the same way detailed talk about the sexual past is often best kept between newcomers and their sponsors, rather than being shared at the meetings. It can sometimes disturb members who are easily offended.

Sex in recovery

Most alcoholics feel quite a lot of anxiety about sex now that they are sober. Many have never had sex without having a drink first. Completely sober sex is thus a new experience which can be frightening. Many male alcoholics have been impotent during their drinking life and many women, because of their drinking, have had few if any orgasms and don't know what it's all about.

If you are single it is not a good idea to rush into a sexual relationship. Newly recovering alcoholics find the emotional side of a love affair very hard to handle and find themselves heading for disaster in short order. In some ways alcoholics only a few months off the drink are rather like teenagers. They become passionately infatuated very easily and when the love affair breaks up, as such affairs are inclined to do, the pain is very hard to bear.

Newly recovering alcoholics should avoid close relationships for the first year in recovery. This is nothing to do with being straitlaced; it is simply that the drama and pain of a love affair are too much. Rushing into love affairs is usually prompted by a desperate need to be loved but it may result in a return to drinking if the emotional side of it is too upsetting.

It's also a good idea not to get involved emotionally or sexually with other recovering alcoholics for the first year of recovery. Very well-balanced alcoholics who have been sober many years don't go out with newcomers. Those who tend to do so are the less healthy members of the fellowship and should be avoided for that very reason. You don't need a sick relationship.

Apart from anything else, keeping away from relationships for the first year helps you to concentrate on recovery – and in the first year, above everything else, this is where your energies should be centred.

Getting comfortable with sex

Many alcoholics take time to feel comfortable with sex. Those who are married or who have a relationship find that making love without a drink, virtually for the first time in their lives, is terrifying. Shyness and embarrassment are extremely common. Often they are frightened of sex, particularly if demeaning sex was part of their drinking life. In reaction to this alcoholics sometimes become unnecessarily puritanical about love-making.

Partners are not always enthusiastic about resuming a sex life because they have been so hurt and damaged by the drinker's behaviour. Many wives and husbands have been so deeply wounded by the experience of living with an alcoholic who was drinking that it may be months before they can trust them again – and good love-making usually needs trust.

Recovering alcoholics have to learn that the ability to 'screw' has nothing to do with love-making. Sexual love requires not just sexual gymnastics but tenderness, care, control and emotional generosity. These qualities are usually conspicuously absent in alcoholic drinkers. It is these qualities that will please any partner and make love-making into what it should be. The earth need not always move. Sometimes love-making is just a question of comfort, cuddles, fun, satisfaction, rather than ecstasy all the time.

Women alcoholics sometimes need to learn to be assertive rather than passive in their sexual lives. If you did not dare to ask for what you want you may feel resentful that your partner did not do it. Make your needs clear. It will help you to have a normal and healthy sex life.

In the same way you are entitled to say no. This word is nothing to be afraid of and as you are recovering from your illness you have regained the right to do only what you feel is good for you. You and your body deserve respect.

Masturbation is another sexual activity which worries alcoholics in recovery, both male and female. In the first year of recovery, when an alcoholic is trying to stay away from emotional relationships, masturbation may be a sexual resource which can help sexual frustration.

Gay men and women

Recovery involves getting honest in all areas of your life. Many gay women and men have found it hard to come to terms with their homosexuality and have to pretend that they are heterosexual. The disordered sex life so common in alcoholics may mean they have been untrue to themselves, taking refuge in a phoney heterosexuality. Other gay men and women have taken up a cruising lifestyle, going from partner to partner and never maintaining any kind of relationship.

Often becoming sober prompts them to accept their homosexuality for the first time. In big cities there are usually gay AA meetings. In ordinary meetings there are many sober, gay men and women who help those who are coming to terms with their own sexuality.

Getting extra help

Sometimes recovering alcoholics remain unhappy with their sexuality. Sexual compulsiveness and sexual obsession do not always die away when the alcohol is put down. They may persist into recovery and it can be a form of addiction itself.

The Twelve Step programme of AA can be used to deal with sexual problems. So can the twenty-four-hour plan of staying away from sex that is degrading for just one day. The housecleaning involved in the fourth and fifth steps of AA helps enormously.

If this is not enough and you need extra help from a therapist ask around in AA to see if they can recommend one who understands the Twelve Step programme. If not there are organisations listed in Appendix 3 which could help.

Any major sexual difficulties between partners can also be tackled by counselling. Bringing these problems into the open with the help of a trained counsellor often diminishes them or does away with them altogether. Indeed all important sexual anxieties are probably best brought into the open in this way.

Some alcoholics have been the victims of incest in the past, particularly children in alcoholic families. Facing this will mean that the past begins to lose its power to hurt and frighten you and to damage your relationships as an adult.

Finding a partner

Many young and single people want to find someone they can live with in a loving relationship. There is absolutely no reason why alcoholics once they have developed some emotional maturity should not fall in love, marry and have children.

This will probably involve relearning the basis of getting acquainted because recovering alcoholics are not usually at ease in drinking places like pubs and clubs when they are in recovery. There are plenty of places where boy meets girl. There are dances, holidays, evening classes. There are sports clubs, restaurants, concerts both pop and classical, church and synagogue groups. But the most obvious place is at work.

How to make contact with new people is something that most young people learn in their teens. Those who have turned to alcohol may never have learned this. So be prepared to feel a little shyness as you begin to lead a normal life.

Of course, you also meet plenty of people in the AA meetings and many AA people do marry each other successfully. However it is risky taking up with an alcoholic who has been clean and sober for *less* than two years as you may find yourself caught up with a drinking alcoholic, and that would be no fun at all. Some counsellors take the view that even sober alcoholics should think carefully about marrying and having children as addiction seems to be passed on genetically and you may be giving your children a double dose of the addiction gene.

Sometimes the search for a partner can become obsessional. 'If only I could find the right person to love then all my problems would be over,' thinks the alcoholic. This is pretty unhealthy, because it means they are looking for a person to solve their problems just as their alcohol used to. This is a bad start to any relationship and likely to end in misery. It is important to remember that depending on a person for your happiness is unhealthy, no matter how reliable, kind and caring that person is. Only when you can live happily with yourself and when your self-worth comes from within are you fit to live happily with another.

Alcoholics and illness

On the whole recovering alcoholics are pretty healthy once they have been away from alcohol from a year or so. Nevertheless if they do become ill, many of them worry about what drugs and medicines they should take. The guiding rule is: only take drugs which are legitimately prescribed for a real illness by a doctor who knows about your alcoholism.

All alcoholics should explain their history to any doctor or dentist treating them. They should also tell any hospital authorities that need to know. For instance alcoholics need larger doses of anaesthetics to put them out.

Be specific about your alcohol use and how long you have been sober. Tell the doctor you need to avoid any mood-altering drugs because as a recovering alcoholic you will have a real likelihood of becoming addicted to any mood-altering substance.

This means keeping away from tranquillisers and sleeping pills, which sometimes doctors quite freely prescribe.

If taking any liquid medicine, check with the chemist as to whether it has an alcohol base. Stick to an aspirin, soluble or otherwise, if you have a temperature and also if you need a pain-killer. If you are prescribed pain-killers in a hospital after an operation, don't take them home with you afterwards. If there is a legitimate medical condition for which you need pain-killers, take the minimum – and keep your sponsor aware of what you are doing. Collect small prescriptions rather than one large prescription for several weeks.

Unfortunately not all doctors understand alcoholism. Quite unknowingly they will prescribe unsuitable medicines, even though you have told them you are a recovering alcoholic. Many alcoholics have been prescribed cough medication which has a large proportion of alcohol in it. It would be wise not to use it, so go back to your doctor and ask him to suggest something else.

Most family doctors are only too delighted when alcoholics become sober as they have usually been a nuisance for years. There remain some, however, who simply do not understand dependence and who may become irritated with alcoholics trying to avoid mood-altering drugs. It is probably best to find another doctor who understands than to stay with the doctor who isn't sympathetic. Local AA members will know of sympathetic practitioners.

Make use of alternative rather than traditional medicine if you think it will help. A list can be found in Appendix 3. But avoid therapies that are run by cults or pushed by high-pressure sales technique. Faddist or extreme diets should also be avoided.

Just like ordinary people, recovering alcoholics sometimes develop other emotional disorders which require help. Get that help from a counsellor or therapist who understands alcoholism, so that your underlying difficulties can be tackled. It is always better to try and talk your problems away, rather than to medicate them away. You will find other AA members know of therapists they have found useful. Ask around in meetings.

Insomnia

Insomnia is one of the commonest side-effects of withdrawal from alcohol. So expect some sleepless nights in the first few months after coming off alcohol.

Although people never die from lack of sleep, being awake can be very wearing and also very boring. Usually the person lies in bed, worrying and staring into the blackness, or pacing around trying to while away the hours. Getting through your sleepless night will be easier if you try to stay in bed. Nobody sleeps vertical, so stay horizontal. A pleasant book that's not too exciting – and a good bedside light – will help to while away the hours. Some people find that it's a good time to read their AA literature to calm the mind. A hot drink sometimes helps.

If you are more than six months off alcohol and are still not sleeping well, it's worth taking measures to deal with your insomnia. As a first step keep a diary to see if there is any pattern.

For some women, insomnia is linked to hormonal changes in the body. Just knowing this makes it easier to bear. There is also a comfort in knowing that as the difficult days pass the period of sleeplessness will come to an end.

Here are some of the things you can do to deal with insomnia:

1. *Follow a fixed routine*. If you don't get up till noon it is foolish to expect your body to fall asleep before midnight. A chaotic lifestyle of late mornings and late nights with no set pattern of sleeping and waking will make it much more difficult. Get up at a normal hour, no matter how sleepless the night has been, and try to develop a pattern of going to bed before midnight and getting up reasonably early so that the body will develop a pattern.

2. *Go to bed earlier*. Some people cannot fall asleep till late because they have not allowed themselves to wind down. Many people need half an hour to wind themselves down at the end of the day, pottering about, tidying up and generally moving towards the bedroom. If you are taking late-night phone calls, working till late or staying active until the last minute you will find it very hard to wind down and sleep. So start moving towards bed a little earlier.

3. *Avoid coffee, tea and drinks with caffeine after 6.00 p.m.*. It's worth remembering that cola and many other canned drinks have a huge caffeine content. Try malted milk or hot black currant.

4. *Take exercise during the day*. Some people make a routine of swimming or doing a work-out in a gym after sedentary work. Physical tiredness, unlike emotional exhaustion, promotes healthy sleep.

5. *Keep the bed warm*. Hot-water bottles, heating pads, bed socks,

electric blankets – don't despise them. Most bodies heat up just before slumber. If you make sure your body is warm you may sleep more easily.

6. *Try meditation.* Methods of relaxation taught in relaxation classes can be practised last thing at night. Relaxation tapes which you can listen to with an earplug so that you do not disturb your partner can also be helpful.

7. *Earplugs to cut down noise and an eye mask to cut out light can also help.*

Insomnia sometimes reflects the emotional well-being. Those who are seriously depressed often wake early in the morning. They need help with their depression, and then their insomnia will often diminish. Likewise those who are angry, anxious or not at peace with themselves may find it difficult. Getting to meetings, confiding your problems to your sponsor and trying to help others can put the mind at rest. A quiet mind is more likely to sleep well.

It must be admitted that some people probably have a naturally high level of alertness, and in them sleeplessness may persist, whatever measures are taken. If you are one of these people, then just accept it. Try to get rest in bed, in comfortable surroundings, with a radio or a good book, even if you cannot sleep. Fighting it will just make you more uptight and more uncomfortable. Just accept that perhaps you are one of those people who need only a few hours sleep, and then you can relax.

14

A Healthy Mind

If you want to be happy as well as free from alcohol you will need to do a lot of work on yourself. As we have said, to lead a happy life you will have to alter many of your attitudes. Let's have a look at this business of changing attitudes. It is at the heart of successful recovery.

By now, if you have been sober for a while, chances are that all kinds of feelings are coming back. Some of these are pleasant – joy, laughter, caring. Others are very disturbing. These are feelings like anger, envy, self-pity and anxiety. Sometimes these feelings just fester away – you are not even sure what they really are.

Recognition and identification

If you are feeling unhappy or ill at ease, the first thing to do is to look at yourself and say, 'What is going on? What do I feel right now?'

Recognition and identification of the emotion is the key.

Are you anxious? Perhaps things are not going right in your life and you are worrying about the future. Are you resentful? Are you chewing something over in your head that makes you feel really angry?

Now admit it. One of the reasons why people stay uncomfortable is that they don't admit to the feelings. They deny they have them or they minimise them or pretend that if they don't talk about them, they will go away.

Once you have admitted what it is that you are feeling you can get rid of those feelings by talking about them in meetings, phoning your sponsor and in general getting them out into the open and dumping them. But these measures, excellent though they are, are only temporary. In the long term, in order to lead a contented life, you must take action to prevent these nasty negative feelings arising in the first place.

What makes people have bad feelings?

Your attitudes inside yourself induce bad feelings like fear, anger and anxiety. 'Rubbish,' you say, 'I'm angry because my parents behave badly.' 'I'm envious because Joe has got a better job than me.' 'As for being anxious, who wouldn't be anxious about getting another job in a society where jobs are few and far between?'

Like most people alcoholics feel that outside things cause uncomfortable feelings, but this isn't really the case. *It's your attitude to people, places and things which causes bad feelings.*

The wrong attitude

Let's say that there are two recovering alcoholics, both of them in their first six months of recovery and both of them out looking for a job. They both go along for interviews, they have both sent their CV ahead of time, they both look good – but in fact neither of them gets the job they are after. Now one of these people goes home, miserable, frustrated, angry, blaming the employer, feeling sorry for himself and saying it's because he is an alcoholic that he doesn't have any luck. He is full of self-pity and very soon he goes back to drinking.

The other alcoholic looks at the situation, accepts it's the first job interview he has been to, and accepts that he may need to learn how to present himself better. He hasn't applied for a job for years, because of his drinking, so he goes home, rewords his CV, gets some advice from friends about how to present himself at interviews and says he will try again.

As you can see, the situations are the same but the attitudes are different. And because their attitudes are so different their emotions and reactions are different too. One was sorry for himself and angry, the other was willing to try again. One went back to alcohol because he couldn't stand the pain of not being able to deal with his feelings of rejection, the other stayed sober.

You make yourself feel bad

It is your thinking that makes you miserable. It is your mind and its attitudes that make you afraid or anxious or resentful or envious or full of self-pity, and it's this attitude that makes you unhappy.

The world doesn't owe the alcoholic anything

Another problem with alcoholics is getting away from the idea that they are a special case, that because they have suffered a painful and damaging illness, somehow the world owes them something. Maybe they feel that they are owed a good relationship or a good marriage or a good job now that they are sober.

They also tell themselves that, because they don't get everything exactly *when* they want it, somehow they are worthless and hopeless. What's the point? All these feelings and attitudes are irrational.

There is nothing in the world which says that alcoholics are entitled to special treatment. Indeed there is nothing in the world that says life's joys and sorrows are going to be distributed fairly. Who said that life was fair?

It is irrational to let yourself think that if things don't go the way you want you can drink again. Because who will suffer? Not the firm that failed to give you a job. But you. You are the one who will suffer.

Finally, the healthy attitude to disappointment is the one that gets on with trying. Keep at it. Don't give up. As the old adage says, 'If at first you don't succeed, try, try and try again'.

Changing attitudes

Changing your attitudes will make you happier. It really will. Here are one or two healthy attitudes that would help you to accept life as it is and not as you would like it to be.

1. *Accept that life isn't fair*. It isn't fair to anybody. If you are feeling particularly sorry for yourself ask yourself if you would like to live

in a country where there was famine and misery. Ask yourself if you would like to be spending the rest of your life in a wheelchair.

2. *Set yourself some practical goals.* If you can't get what you want, start wanting what you can get. Recovery is about learning to live with the reality you have, not changing reality to suit you. And that means being realistic. Set yourself reachable goals not unreachable ones, so that you are not always disappointed or always putting yourself down.

3. *Allow yourself to be wrong.* Everyone is wrong at some time and, what's more, many of these mistakes are valuable. Think it out. You learn more from mistakes than from successes.

4. *Leave the words 'should' or 'ought' out of your vocabulary.* They have nothing to do with reality.

5. *Stop dramatising the situation.* Isn't it awful, terrible, disastrous, frightful, scary? Really? Is anything in your life awful compared with living south of the Sahara and having the prospect of dying before you are five. Or spending your life in the shadow of a volcano, where a few years ago you watched your family being wiped out by volcanic lava. Every time you exaggerate, bring yourself back to reality by trying to see things in their proper perspective.

6. *Let go of making yourself feel bad.* If you have a problem that is scary or worrying you, take a good look at it, identify it, ask yourself if there is anything you can do about it and, if there isn't, just dump it.

7. *See things from other people's point of view.* Alcoholics are inclined to be very self-centred. Stop thinking you are the centre of the universe and start looking at things from other people's point of view.

8. *Don't expect too much from other people.* People who are not alcoholics also have their problems, their fears and their worries. They are not saints, and some people in the world are just as emotionally ill as you, sometimes worse.

9. *Don't let others wind you up.* You can choose the way you react just as well as you can choose anything else. If somebody picks a fight with you, you don't have to respond in kind. You don't have to pick up on their anger, you can respond in a caring way. It is a great diffuser.

Family reactions

Don't be put out if your family greet with scepticism or even downright disbelief the wonderful news that you are in AA and recovering a day at a time. And you may find that they are still checking up on you or treating you as if you were still drinking.

Before you get upset, think about it from their point of view. Months, sometimes years, of pressure on the family have caused them to become emotionally damaged themselves. They have listened to the endless lies you told them while you were drinking. They have heard your promises many times before and they've been through the despair of realising your promises would not be kept.

Why should they believe you now? Don't coax or bully them into understanding. But encourage them to go to Al-anon; as the months pass and you stay sober and get on with your recovery, their scepticism will disappear and they will be thrilled to see you changing before their very eyes.

Learning to care for others

Sometimes as you get more and more sober, you see that other people in your family have problems too. Maybe you will notice that your wife has become dependent on tranquillisers, trying to cope with your problems. Maybe you will see that your child is hooked on marijuana or heroin and you never saw it happening because you were too immersed in your own drinking and your own problems.

Helping other alcoholics

You have to be careful that you don't start preaching immediately you are off the bottle. You have to show by example that life can be different. This is a recovery of attraction, not of just telling other people how to do it. It may be very hard to hold your tongue when you think you know the answers. Sometimes it takes time and it needs tact to steer people into recovery.

Relapses after long-term sobriety

Unfortunately, alcoholism is a relapsing illness. No matter how long you have been sober the susceptibility to relapse always remains.

An alcoholic is never cured

Relapses most often occur when alcoholics begin to take sobriety for granted. They stop going to AA meetings or, if they continue to attend, they can't be bothered to contribute. A good way to avoid complacency is to get involved in helping alcoholics who are still drinking.

There is a quick check you can run on yourself if you begin to feel a bit smug about AA. Ask yourself the following questions

1. *Do I have a home AA group?* If not, why not? There is a great advantage in regular attendance at the same AA meeting. You can get close to people and, because they know you well, they'll notice if your thinking is moving away from the Twelve Step programme. This way you may get a warning in time to stop you relapsing.

2. *Do I keep in regular touch with my sponsor?* The idea of having a sponsor is to be in regular touch with somebody who has successfully come off drink, who understands the problems of recovery and who can help you in the difficult times. It's no good having a sponsor whom you don't see or talk to. A sponsor is someone who will tell you what you *need* to know about yourself. If you haven't got a sponsor, does it mean that you don't want somebody to know all about you?

3. *Are you working the Twelve Steps?* If you have decided you can do without them, you are risking much misery, unhappiness, loneliness and dissatisfaction. Is there something in your life you are not feeling good about? Anger and resentment, self-pity, guilty secrets or sick behaviour could all be signs that you are heading for trouble.

4. *What are you doing for the alcoholic who is still suffering?* Helping other alcoholics is an essential part of recovery. They have a saying in AA – you keep your recovery by giving it away. You can do this by helping out on Twelve Step calls, which means going out and talking to people who are trying to stop. Doing volunteer phone duty, helping to run a meeting, helping with the literature, taking care of the tea and the coffee, or even putting out the chairs for the meeting. Simple, practical things – and if you don't do these things you are putting your sobriety at risk. Not being involved means that you might be drifting away. Involvement in any club means service, to be a giver and not the taker that you may have always been.

Staying off and keeping happy

You do not have to relapse. Many people never take another drink from the first day that they go into recovery. You will often find people who have enjoyed twenty or thirty years of sobriety.

As you get to know these people you will discover that they are action people. They are doers not talkers. They have taken the principles of recovery into their daily lives and applied them in every area of their life, with determination and good humour. The best AA members are the ones who can laugh at themselves, who are unpompous, unstuffy, positive and normal.

Most people who come into AA have no idea how much happiness awaits them. Recovery isn't fast. Many alcoholics get very impatient and want it all fixed today. It takes years rather than months really to find that peace of mind which you see around you. But in time most people feel remarkably happy. Many people in AA are in fact much happier than people who do not even have this illness because they learn a way of life to deal with feelings and emotions that ordinary people never meet.

You can be one of them.

PART SIX

For Social Workers, Teachers, Employers and Members of the Helping Professions

15

Helping the Alcoholic to Recover or to Stay Ill?

Alcoholism is an enormous problem in our society. At a conservative estimate there are at least **750,000** alcoholics in the UK.

Doctors, magistrates, social workers, solicitors, probation officers, voluntary workers, clergymen, occupational health workers, personnel managers, marriage guidance counsellors and union officials will all have to deal with the problems caused by alcoholism. Sadly, many of these professions have little if any real knowledge of alcoholism. Their training either ignores the issue altogether or puts forward out-of-date ideas about it. No wonder individuals feel upset, frustrated and irritated when they have to deal with alcoholics.

The view that alcoholics are weak or bad or moral degenerates doesn't help this problem. Very few people in the caring professions really accept this as a treatable illness as they have little or no experience of the disease and many have never come into contact with recovering alcoholics. Recovering alcoholics are, by the nature of their recovery, anonymous and therefore invisible.

Ignoring the problem

Many professionals have had no training in recognising the problem in the first place. They are inclined to see the alcoholic still as the skid-row bum or the pathetic lady in the street carrying all her worldly goods in a plastic bag. Instead they should recognise that the majority of alcoholics are young to middle-aged, employed and with families. They are bright, over-sensitive and achievers, before they lose out in all areas of their lives because of their drinking.

The professionals may concentrate all their efforts in helping people with their behavioural or environmental problems such as housing, money or family, without seeing that these problems are the results of drinking, not the causes of the drinking problem. Sadly, our society itself refuses to recognise the early stages of drink dependence. As we have said, it is much more comfortable for most of us to think of the alcoholic as the meths drinker living rough rather than as the successful company director whose work is increasingly erratic but whose diagnosis is put down as executive stress, because nobody – his doctor, his colleagues, his family – want to recognise that his drinking has changed his behaviour.

Indeed, society ignores the problems of alcoholism altogether. While the media constantly has headlines about drug problems, there is much less concern about drink. *Yet for every addict there are twenty alcoholics in our society, most of whom have suffering families.*

Recognising the problem in its early stages

Alcoholism is a progressive illness which over the years robs sufferers of their health, their happiness, their self-respect and often their lives. The longer it goes on the more difficult it is for the alcoholic to recover. In the early stages, as in any illness, recovery is much more easily achieved than when the alcoholism has become chronic. Yet many professional workers either fail to recognise the illness in its early stages or for reasons of social embarrassment, wishful thinking, loyalty or misplaced kindness do not confront the alcoholic. In this way they rob the alcoholic of his or her chance of an early recovery.

Failing to treat the illness in the early stages is not kind to the alcoholic. As we have said, it is like letting a woman with a small lump in her breast go away untreated until it becomes near-terminal. The result is that the alcoholics get more and more damaged and sick. Society gives them permission to continue on the downward path. After all, as people say, 'Everyone has a right to drink.' So they become more and more ill and more and more desperately unhappy.

Recognising the alcoholic

In Chapter 6 we gave the tell-tale signs of alcoholism. For people living in close contact with an alcoholic these signs are helpful. But many professionals are not in such close contact. They may see the alcoholic only in an office, rather than at home, and alcoholics are brilliant at putting on a good front when dealing with authority or with people outside their family.

Asking the family

The best way to find out if there is a drink problem is to involve the family. Ask the wife, the parent, the sister, the brother, the child – because they usually know enough about the relative's way of life to realise what is going on. Though they too may be slow to use the word 'alcoholic' because they also tend to look on the meths drinker as the only alcoholic.

If you are asking a family member, make sure it is someone stable. Alcoholics sometimes marry or live with someone with the same problem. Sometimes a family feels stigmatised by the illness and denies the problem. In many cases if you involve the family in your investigation you will discover the truth. You will not get the truth in most cases from the alcoholic. Either alcoholics don't recognise that their problems stem from their drinking or they will lie and deny the problem to protect themselves and their drinking behaviour. In many cases the family have been suffering for years.

In the later stages of the illness the alcoholic often becomes ill and has difficulties at work or difficulties with the law and these are all pointers to the problem.

Medical signs of alcoholism

Before anybody actually diagnoses alcoholism, other diagnoses may precede it. These include such things as gastritis, stomach ulcers, cirrhosis, pancreatitis, heart disease, peripheral neuro-pathy, anxiety state, depression and even impotence. Even something minor like repeated visits to the doctor for small aches and pains is a warning because it probably means that the alcoholic is trying to get days off work when he or she is feeling lousy. Broken appointments or inappropriate lateness, or sometimes endless inappropriate telephone calls are also a sign of this illness.

Signs of alcoholism at work

Absence from work on Mondays and days after holidays, absence from work on Friday afternoons, undue numerous absences for minor illnesses such as flu or gastric upsets, working during overtime periods to raise extra money for drink, padded expenses, long lunch breaks, lack of concentration or rational thinking after lunch, complaints of stress, decreasing job performance, grandiose behaviour, requests for salary advances and sometimes financial dishonesty are all indications of this illness.

Signs of alcoholism in relationships

Domestic disputes about money, frequent rows at home, late-night phone calls for no good reason, wife battering, baby battering, promiscuous sexual relationships, separation and divorce are all indications of alcoholism.

Problems with the law and alcoholism

'Drunk and disorderly' charges, drunk driving and shoplifting all suggest a problem with alcohol. It is a cluster of these signs rather than any one on its own that is likely to point to alcoholism. For example, not everybody with a stomach ulcer is necessarily an alcoholic, but if there is a medical record of stomach ulcers combined with a conviction for drunk driving you should take a good hard look at this person.

Helping the alcoholic to stay ill

Many professionals spend a great deal of time and energy trying to help the alcoholic in the hope that if they improve their outward circumstances they will do something about the drinking. Professionals are often taken in by the alcoholics' story that if only their lives and circumstances were different then they could drink normally. This is a myth and must be disregarded if you are to get anywhere with the alcoholic. Quite often alcoholics put up a very good case for help. They say, and honestly believe, that they would be more likely to stop drinking if they were in a different environment. This is also a great way of getting people to feel sorry for them.

Sympathy kills

Sympathy is just about the most destructive thing you can give to an alcoholic. Alibis and excuses are a way of life for alcoholics. They are not only conning those around them, they are also desperately conning themselves. The truth is that helping them with their outward circumstances before they stop drinking is a waste of time. Many professionals spend weeks and months on particular cases trying to make things comfortable for the alcoholic and then get frustrated, depressed and sometimes bitter when the alcoholic does nothing.

It is better to say to the alcoholic, 'When you do something about your drinking, then I'll help you with your other problems.' You could avoid a lot of wasted time and effort.

Finding the alcoholic a job

We did not believe this when we first came into contact with alcoholics, even though we were told it. In particular we wasted a lot of time and energy when we were working in vocational rehabilitation in the United States.

When we were put in charge of career problems, our boss in the office told us it was no use helping alcoholics until they had stopped drinking. The time to help them was when they had been off drink for a period of time.

We didn't believe him, we thought we knew better. The alcoholics came to us and said, 'What I need is a job and then I'll get my drinking under control,' and we would go to enormous lengths to help them, giving them tests, looking for opportunities – and at the last minute they wouldn't show.

We began to see we were complete idiots, who were just being sucked in by their hard-luck stories. So we began to approach the problem in the opposite order. First we would find them treatment for the alcohol problem, and then, when they got into recovery, we would find them a job as they came out of treatment. And in that order there was success.

Treating underlying psychological problems

The other great waste of time and effort is to treat alcoholics for their underlying psychological problems while they are still drinking. It is like trying to have a conversation with somebody who is just coming out of an anaesthetic. You wouldn't dream of doing that, but you see no problem in accepting that you can do this with an alcoholic.

It is true that alcoholics display some quite remarkable emotional and behavioural disorders but many of these are the results and not the causes of their drinking. If alcohol is removed, many of the problems fall away. In fact it doesn't make any sense to try and evaluate an alcoholic's emotional problems until they have been sober for a period of time.

Alcoholics sometimes do need therapy for their emotional disorders but they need it after they have stopped drinking, otherwise it is a waste of time and money. It is in sobriety that some of them need professional help to deal with family or emotional problems and to learn how to lead a new and happy life.

No easy solutions

You never lose anything by being forceful or straight up with the alcoholic. If you try and reason or bargain the alcoholic will never respect you and therefore never listen to you. The alcoholic must be told firmly that abstinence from alcohol and any other mood-altering chemical is the only answer. To suggest there might be easier ways just delays the final recovery.

Many professionals try to offer easy solutions, not least because many alcoholics refuse point-blank to do without their alcohol. We all want to be liked by others, even by our clients, therefore there is a strong temptation to back down and not confront an alcoholic with this truth.

As a result alcoholics may be told to try and cut down their drinking rather than to stop altogether – something that they cannot in the long term achieve. They have been trying to do it for years. Many professional people who are social drinkers them-selves simply cannot grasp the idea that for an alcoholic moderation is an unknown quantity.

The advice to the alcoholic to cut down or go without alcohol for a specific period of time with a promise that then he or she will be able to drink again is incorrect. All this does is to make the alcoholic fit enough to drink. It is just what any alcoholic wants to hear, though deep down he or she knows it's a lie.

Quite often when alcoholics are faced with this truth they react with anger and self-pity. This is part of the denial system we have already described which is characteristic of almost all alcoholics.

Helping the alcoholic to recover

It takes personal courage on your part to tell alcoholics that their drinking will get worse and worse unless they stop altogether. It also takes courage to refuse to 'help' unless they do something serious about their drinking – yet refusing to help is the kindest thing you can do. In the long term it is no help just to paint over the rust.

Getting to know AA

When an alcoholic is willing to stop drinking, it is important strongly to recommend frequent attendance at AA. A lukewarm or half-hearted suggestion will be ineffective. Research has shown that when the therapist or counsellor or helping professional warmly and firmly recommends these organisations the alcoholic is much more likely to follow the recommendation. Remember, alcoholics need help not just to stop but to stay stopped for ever on a 'day at a time' basis.

Alcoholics Anonymous is not just for last-hope cases, nor is it solely for middle-class clients. These myths abound because a staggering number of those who deal with alcoholics have never gone to AA and have no idea how it works.

We believe that those who treat alcoholics or their problems should go to at least twenty AA meetings. Anything less that this means that they miss the opportunity of learning how to help others. You must familiarise yourself with this organisation, with how it works and with the kind of people you meet.

AA has open meetings at which outsiders are welcome. All you need to do is ring the phone number in Appendix 2 and get the details. It is unprofessional to let embarrassment and shyness or even laziness get in the way of doing this.

You can also build up a network of AA contacts in the local area which can help you a great deal when dealing with your clients.

Those who have only occasional dealings with alcoholics should also get the addresses and phone numbers of the AA meetings. When they have done this they will be in a much better position to give help. In fact most professionals who go to these meetings find themselves absolutely fascinated.

You will find some clients go to just one AA meeting and come back and say, 'Oh, that's not for me, there was nobody there like me.' 'It all sounds holier than thou.' At this point, don't back off and say, 'Yes, I know it is difficult.' Just encourage them to keep going. They wouldn't join a sports club or any other kind of club and just go once and say it was no good. They'd go at least half a dozen times to make sure the place was right for them.

How the law can help

At the moment many alcoholics come up in the courts on a variety of charges related to their drinking. Many of them commit acts which rightly earn them prison sentences, yet the law usually avoids helping them to do anything about their drinking.

Some states in the US have arrangements whereby drunk drivers have to attend a course on alcohol and alcoholism. They learn about drinking and about the symptoms of alcoholism. Those among them who have a drink problem are encouraged to get help.

Judges may sentence the offender to a course of, say, thirty AA meetings or to a specific course of rehabilitation in a treatment centre as an alternative to a fine or imprisonment.

None of these sentencing alternatives usually happen in Britain. Magistrates can and often do recommend AA from the Bench, but it seldom goes beyond a personal suggestion.

Nearly all prisons in Britain have a regular meeting of AA. If you are a probation officer, prison visitor or magistrate it is imperative to *suggest* these meetings to the offender. A very high proportion of men and women in prison are there because of alcohol-related offences. We believe it would be money well spent to set up programmes for alcoholics within the prison system. As it is, too many of these ill people receive no help at all and come out of prison only to go back to alcohol. And soon they commit more crimes caused by their drinking.

Society is the loser as much as the alcoholic when the illness goes untreated.

You are doing no favour to the alcoholic to let him escape the consequences of his drinking. Prison sentences are rightly given to those who commit serious crime, no matter what the reason.

Don't accept the excuse 'I could not help what I was doing because I was sick'. In a sense this is true, the crime took place under the influence of alcohol. But sometimes experiencing the results of their drinking is the only way that alcoholics really begin to see that they have a problem with alcohol.

Helping or protecting alcoholics simply enables them to go on drinking.

Helping the alcoholic family

If you can help family members around the alcoholic, then do so. It is really the families who are the victims, not the alcoholics, and they have often suffered severely. Physically, financially and emotionally, there is endless abuse.

Children in particular are always at risk in an alcoholic home. It is not that their parents do not care, it is simply that the chaos surrounding the alcoholic affects all their lives. As we have already described, their lives are, above all, emotionally chaotic. The alcoholic parent is one moment kind and loving and the next an angry, disappointing, promise-breaking stranger. There is no emotional security.

Physical and sometimes sexual abuse does happen and fear is the constant companion of the child in the alcoholic household.

It is important that children should be told about alcoholism. That way they have some idea of why these things are happening. Without this knowledge some children believe that in some way they are at fault, and many make pathetic efforts to put it right. If they are told about the illness of alcoholism, even quite young children readily understand and it makes sense to them. This will relieve them of the burden of misplaced responsibility and release them from their feelings of fear, guilt and anger, which sometimes amount to hate.

Al-anon and Alateen

The fellowships Al-anon and Alateen, the family organisations associated with AA, are crucial. They can do a great deal to help the suffering family, whether or not the alcoholic stops drinking.

Once again a surprising number of professionals don't even know about these organisations and have certainly never been to a meeting. They are in almost total ignorance of what they do and how they do it. Without seeing for yourself you may, in the words of some marriage counsellors who had never bothered to investigate for themselves, believe that the meetings are just 'tea and coffee chat sessions'.

Both Al-anon and Alateen give enormous help to suffering families, who often bear the brunt of the bad behaviour of the alcoholic. Al-anon is specifically for wives, families and friends of the alcoholic and Alateen is for the children of alcoholics. In some cities there is also ACA for adult children of alcoholics, to help them deal with the legacy of their disturbed past. All these organisations are listed in Appendix 2. Just ring and get the address of the nearest meeting.

Help from schools

Teachers and schools can play an important part in educating people about alcohol. All the self-help groups we have mentioned will provide speakers who will help you to understand the problems.

Most children will find it a good deal more interesting to hear this from somebody who has *had* the illness and recovered.

There is also literature available from the head offices of these organisations. Older teenagers should be encouraged to find out for themselves by going to an open meeting as part of a school project. Literature, films and speakers can also be provided.

Finally schools need to remember that drinking starts at a very young age. We have treated children as young as fourteen, who have been drinking up to a bottle of spirits a day and whose lives are as a result wrecked. Some of the children attending school already have quite a severe alcohol problem but it is hidden, and quite deliberately so. Like all alcoholics they need help at the early stages, not later, and like all alcoholics total abstinence is the answer. The sooner the message reaches them the better their chance of recovery.

Treatment programme at Farm Place

What we have done in our programme is to integrate the caring philosophy of AA into a professional treatment programme. This is a team concept, including counselling, nursing, medical, psychological and psychiatric staff who have had special training and experience with the disease of alcoholism.

In doing this, something profound seems to have occurred: a humanising of a complex treatment programme with the close sharing found in Alcoholics Anonymous and Al-anon.

Perhaps the most important factor in the programme is the opportunity the patient has to learn and grow in small structured groups. There is an immediate effectiveness in the sharing of a common experience.

In simple terms, people who have made a career of abusing alcohol, and who have been dishonest, manipulative and destructive towards their families and friends, learn to change when confronted with each other and with their common chronic dependence.

In Dr Ernest Kurtz's book on the history of AA there is a vivid description of the experience of finding this common identity. Dr Kurtz writes of 'the shared honesty and the mutual vulnerability openly acknowledged'. This suggests that if alcoholics can give up trying to be grandiose or omnipotent as a cover for fear and guilt, and admit their limitations, this admission will provide the dynamic which makes change and recovery possible.

From this acceptance of limitation they can rejoin the human race and find a common mutual humanity. This spiritual experience encourages the alcoholic to find the courage to face up to his illness and to recover.

The primary function of any dependency programme is to evaluate and initiate proper treatment for people who are suffering from alcohol dependence. A wide range of services are provided by the treatment team. We think very few if any professionals can work with this illness successfully outside a team. It is just too draining and emotionally stressful.

Based on the patient's history, current physical and emotional state, employment and family situation, a referral may be made to the out-patient department at our London centre or at Farm Place, our treatment centre in Ockley, Surrey. Some are directly admitted to in-patient treatment at Farm Place. We insist on involvement in AA both during and after treatment.

Out-patient treatment begins with a medical assessment and detoxification, followed by the necessary therapy by counselling, group therapy and family counselling, as indicated by the individual treatment plan which is developed by the treatment team.

The patient requiring in-patient treatment receives a full medical examination and is placed on a detoxification regimen if necessary. In order to assist the newly admitted patient to understand the programme there is an introductory and orientation session, explaining the structure of the programme and the patient's responsibilities and rights while in treatment. Soon after admission each patient is assessed several times so that an individual treatment plan can be developed. Treatment designs are based on a series of interviews with the patient, supplemented by the co-operation of the family, GP, employers and other significant people in the patient's life.

This plan is designed to enable each individual to progress according to his or her capabilities. All patients have frequent sessions of individual counselling to enable them to recognise their dependence on alcohol and the resultant damage, and to resolve problems relating to the special needs of each individual and his or her family.

Structured group therapy takes place twice daily. By sharing their experiences patients can come to terms with their dependence on alcohol and the damage it has caused to themselves and others. With the support of their peers patients face their mutual problems with alcohol and begin to change.

Families are encouraged to involve themselves in the treatment programme. They participate in multiple family groups and individual family counselling sessions. This is to ensure that the family members understand the nature of alcoholism.

Individual treatment plans are developed by the team for all families to maximise their involvement. This is sometimes described as the Families System Approach to Alcoholism. In recent years it has been recognised how much families of alcoholics have become emotionally damaged by association with the illness. The patient has often blamed his need for alcohol on his or her family. Many are taken in by this. They have taken the blame on themselves and have become immobilised or complicit in the illness.

Family Programmes must therefore be geared to teach the family to modify their reactions and to detach themselves from the patient while still caring for him or her.

Another aim is to help the family to know what to expect when the patient comes home. They must learn to live for themselves and not to adapt to the mood of the dependent person. They must accept that their own personal growth is good for them and that what is good for them is good for the alcoholic.

Patients also participate in the self-help groups of AA while in treatment and these become their support system when they are in recovery.

This also applies to family members in Al-anon, Alateen and ACA. Early in treatment each patient is given a psychological assessment, which is communicated directly to him or her in a comprehensible way. This is to help the patient to develop insight and understanding into the psychological problems that develop as the alcoholism progresses, and to see how these problems usually recede as recovery stabilises.

Patients are also assessed to make sure that they suffer from no serious psychiatric problem related to or even independent of alcoholism. This assessment is integrated into the individual treatment plan and updated as appropriate.

Further information is given to patients during treatment in the form of lectures and discussions about different aspects of alcoholism: physical and emotional guidelines for recovery, ways of coping, and how the role of the family will change in recovery.

Exercise and relaxation sessions are provided to enhance the patient's physical and emotional well-being and also to promote social interaction. Having fun without alcohol is often a new experience, which must be learned or relearned after years during which alcohol has been the main social lubricant.

Some patients need a longer period of treatment than four to eight weeks in primary care. Extended care is provided within the residential centre at Farm Place, when the aim is to help patients make changes in lifestyle and attitudes and to develop self-worth without the risk of returning to alcohol.

Some patients who have a long alcoholic history, or with a previous history of extensive relapse, need to spend between six months and one year in a half-way house to consolidate recovery in a structured environment. A half-way house provides counselling and group therapy as well as opportunities to work, to continue education and to progress to normal living while involvement in AA is developing.

Plans are made to ensure as far as possible that the patient has the best chance of recovery. After-care services include introduction to the appropriate self-help group, out-patient follow-up and group therapy. The main goal of after-care is to continue progress made in treatment and to work towards handling the problems of normal living. We monitor the progress of all patients for at least five years.

Recovery really begins when patients return home to use the tools they have acquired during treatment and the skills they will continue to learn with the assistance of AA.

Our success rate

Those who specialise in the treatment of alcoholism know that it is not easy to treat alcoholics. The most important British study of the 1980s at an eminent London hospital followed up one hundred alcoholics from stable family and work backgrounds at intervals of six, twelve, eighteen and twenty-four months after hospital in-patient treatment. It showed that after two years there was a 100 per cent relapse rate. All the patients have gone back to drinking.

Our treatment results are much better. Our follow-up studies cover all patients including even those who didn't fully complete treatment and they range from the very young to alcoholics in their sixties. All patients were followed up at six-month intervals for five years after treatment.

Conservatively, fifty of every hundred patients were totally abstinent and the quality of their lives had improved in most areas.

A further twenty-five per cent had had a relapse, usually of a few days' duration after leaving treatment but had returned to abstinence and had successfully continued in recovery. These short-term relapses were often characteristic of the very young or alcoholics who had left treatment early; although persuaded that they had a drink problem, they nevertheless made one final effort to prove the treatment wrong. Their relapse instead acted as a final convincer that abstinence was the only answer.

The final twenty-five per cent of alcoholics relapsed after treatment and had to be rehospitalised or required further long-term treatment. Among these were many who had left treatment early.

These results show that treating alcoholics is not a waste of time or money and that with the right treatment a high degree of success can be expected. Some patients indeed have an even better prognosis. Referrals by employers or unions with a policy of treatment and support for alcoholism, instead of dismissal or covering up the problem, can expect a 75–80 per cent recovery rate without relapse.

Treating alcoholics is extremely rewarding. We see them arrive as sick, miserable, frightened people leading destructive lives; but as their recovery progresses they become happy, stable, achieving people who have regained their self-respect.

This is a disease, *not* a disgrace. When treated as such the outcome is little short of miraculous.

APPENDIX 1

The Twelve Steps

1. We admitted we were powerless over alcohol, and that our lives had become unmanageable.

2. Came to believe that a Power greater than ourselves could restore us to sanity.

3. Made a decision to turn our will and our lives over to the care of God *as we understood Him.*

4. Made a searching and fearless moral inventory of ourselves.

5. Admitted to God, to ourselves, and to another human being the exact nature of our wrongs.

6. Were entirely ready to have God remove all these defects of character.

7. Humbly asked Him to remove our shortcomings.

8. Made a list of all persons we had harmed, and became willing to make amends to them all.

9. Made direct amends to such people whenever possible, except when to do so would injure them or others.

10. Continued to take personal inventory and when we were wrong promptly admitted it.

11. Sought through prayer and meditation to improve our conscious contact with God *as we understood Him*, praying only for knowledge of His will for us and the power to carry that out.

12. Having had a spiritual awakening as a result of these steps, we tried to carry this message to alcoholics and to practise these principles in all our affairs.

(Reprinted with permission of AA World Services Inc.)

APPENDIX 2

Self-Help Groups and Agencies Dealing With Chemical Dependence

These addresses and telephone numbers were collected at the beginning of 1986. By the time you are reading this book, some of them may have changed. If so, simply look in the phone book for the new number.

Great Britain

Alcoholics Anonymous, PO Box 1, Stonebow House, Stonebow, York YO1 2NJ. Tel: 0904 644026/7/8/9. AA is for anybody who wants to stop drinking. There are local offices in many areas, so consult your local phone book.

Al-anon Family Groups, 61 Great Dover Street, London SE1 4YF. Tel: 01–403 0888. Al-anon is for anybody who has a relative or friend with a drinking problem. It can help those adults who grew up in an alcoholic home. Alateen, its branch for teenagers, helps young people whose parents or relatives have a drinking problem. Local phone books may have a number. AA offices usually will pass this on, if it is not in the book.

Narcotics Anonymous, PO Box 246, London SW10. Tel:

01–351 6794. NA is for anybody who wants to stop using drugs – no matter who they are or what drug they are using, including legally prescribed drugs like tranquillisers and sleeping pills.

Families Anonymous, 88 Caledonian Road, London N1 9DN. Tel: 01–278 8805. FA is for anybody with a relative or friend who is using drugs, including prescribed drugs and glue sniffing. FA will help those who are not yet sure if the problem is one of drugs.

St Bernard's Hospital, Ealing Health Authority, Uxbridge Road, Southall UB1 3EU. NHS hospital.

Warlingham Park Hospital, Warlingham, Surrey. NHS hospital.

Farm Place, Ockley, Surrey RH5 5NG. Tel: 030679 742 (in-patients); 39 Upper Grosvenor Street, London W1. Tel: 01–491 8409 (out-patients). Alcoholism and addiction treatment.

Other agencies

Standing Conference on Drug Abuse, 1–4 Hatton Place, Hatton Garden, London EC1N 8ND. Tel: 01–430 2341. SCODA can supply a list of hospitals which provide a service for drug users, a list of residential rehabilitation places for drug users, and a list of advisory services and day projects for drug users. Send a large stamped addressed envelope for these.

Republic of Ireland

Alcoholics Anonymous, 109 South Circular Road, Dublin 8. Tel: Dublin 538998 (9a.m.–5p.m. Mon.–Fri.); at other times 774809/714050.

Al-anon, 61 Great Dover Street, London SE1 4YF. Tel: 01–403 0888. The London office deals with enquiries about meetings in Eire.

Narcotics Anonymous, PO Box 1368, Sherriff Street, Dublin 1. No Dublin phone number was available in 1985. Phone London NA office on 01–351 6794 for details of local meetings.

Families Anonymous, 88 Caledonian Road, London N1 9DN. Tel: 01–278 8805 for details of meetings in Eire. In 1985 there were FA meetings in Dublin, though the central office was in London.

Australia

Narcotics Anonymous: PO Box 440, Leichandt, New South Wales

2040. Tel: 02–810 2020. There are also other NA offices in other major cities, so check your phone directory to see if there is one near you.

Alcoholics Anonymous, PO Box 5321, Sydney, New South Wales 2001. Tel: 02–290 2210. Also many local AA offices.

Families Anonymous. There is no general office, but in 1985 there was an FA meeting being held in Melbourne. Up-to-date information from Families Anonymous, PO Box 528, Van Nuys, California 91408.

Nar Anon, PO Box Q108, Queen Victoria Building, Sydney, New South Wales 2000. Tel: 02–300 9736. Nar-Anon is another organisation for the families of those addicted to drugs.

Al-anon Family Groups, PO Box 1002H, Melbourne, Victoria 3001. Tel: 03–62 4933.

Other agencies

In so far as there is a national organisation, it is the **Alcohol and Drug Foundation**, PO Box 477, Canberra City, ACT 2601. There are plans for an emergency phone service in all capital cities in the future with a national (008) number.

In addition there are the following state organisations:

New South Wales
Alcohol and Drug Information Service, St Vincent's Hospital, Sydney. Tel: 02–331 2111. 24-hour service of advice and referral.
New South Wales Drug and Alcohol Authority, Level 14, McKell Building, Rawson Place, Sydney, New South Wales 2000.

Victoria
Victorian Foundation on Alcohol and Drug Dependence, PO Box 529, South Melbourne 3205.

Queensland
Alcohol and Drug Dependence Services, 'Biala', 270 Roma Street, Brisbane, Queensland 4000.

South Australia
Drug and Alcohol Services Council, 161 Greenhill Road, Parkside, South Australia 5063.

Western Australia
Western Australian Alcohol and Drug Authority, Salvatori House, 36 Outram Street, West Perth 6005.

Northern Territory
Northern Territory Drug and Alcohol Bureau, PO Box 1701, Darwin 5794.

Canada

Narcotics Anonymous Regional Service Office, 161 Princess Street West, North Bay, Ontario P1B 6C5. Check with the directory for the phone number. Quebec District Office, 1691 Champlain, Shawinigan, Quebec J9N 2K8. Check with the phone directory for the current phone number.

Alcoholics Anonymous, Suite 6, 1581 Bank Street, Ottawa, Ontario K1H 7Z3. Tel: 613 523 9977. There are phone lines for every major city, so look in your local phone directory.

Families Anonymous, PO Box 528, Van Nuys, California 91408. Tel: 213 989 7841. There are several FA meetings in Canada, but the central office is in California.

Al-anon: PO Box 182, Madison Square Station, New York, NY 10159. Tel: 212 683 1771. Check in the phone book to see if there is a local Al-anon number.

Other agencies

Alcoholism Commission of Saskatchewan, 3475 Albert Street, Regina, Saskatchewan S4S 6X6. Tel: 306–565 4085.

Alcohol and Drug Programs, Ministry of Health, 1515 Blanshard Street, Victoria, British Columbia V8V 3C8. Tel: 604 386 3166.

Nova Scotia Commission on Drug Dependency, 5675 Spring Garden Road, Halifax, Nova Scotia B3J 1H1. Tel: 902 424 4270.

Addiction Research Foundation, 33 Russell Street, Toronto, Ontario M5S 3S1. Tel: 416 595 6000.

Alcoholism Foundation of Manitoba, 1031 Portage Avenue, Winnipeg, Manitoba R3G 0R8. Tel: 204 786 3831.

Alcohol and Drug Dependency Commission, 6 Logy Bay Road, St John's, Newfoundland A1A 1J3. Tel: 709 737 3600.

Alcohol and Drug Services, Department of Health and Human Resources, Box 2703, Whitehorse, Yukon Y1A 2C6. Tel: 403 667 5777.

Addiction Services, Department of Health, PO Box 37, Charlotte-town, Prince Edward Island C1A 7K2. Tel: 902 892 4265.

Alcoholism and Drug Dependency Commission of New Bruns-wick, 43 Brunswick Street, Fredericton, New Brunswick E3B 5H1. Tel: 506 453 2136.

Alberta Alcoholism and Drug Abuse Commission, 7th Floor, 10909 Jasper Avenue, Edmonton, Alberta T5J 3M9. Tel: 403 427 7305.

Alcohol and Drug Program, PO Box 1769, Yellowknife, North-west Territories X1A 2L9. Tel: 403 873 7707.

New Zealand

Narcotics Anonymous. PO Box 2858, Christchurch. No fixed telephone number at the time of this book's publication in 1986. Check in your local phone book. Sometimes AA offices have an NA contact number. Or get in touch with the Narcotics Anony-mous head office, 16155 Wyandotte Street, Van Nuys, California 91406. Or telephone the NA Australasian region head office in Australia: 02–810 2020.

Alcoholics Anonymous, PO Box 6458, Wellington, NI. Tel: 859 455.

Families Anonymous. In 1985 there were not yet meetings of FA in New Zealand. For up-to-date information write to Families Anonymous, PO Box 528, Van Nuys, California 91408. If your addict uses alcohol (and most do) you can get help from Al-anon.

Al-anon, Suite no 4, Charter House, 56 Customs Street, Auckland. Tel: Auckland 794–871

Other agencies

The Drugs Advisory Committee, Department of Health, Macarthy Trust Building, Lambton Quay, Wellington. Tel: 727 627. This committee advises the Minister of Health on drug abuse. It has a list of treatment and rehabilitation centres.

South Africa

Narcotics Anonymous. In 1986 there were reports of a very small

NA community in South Africa, but without an office. The main office of Alcoholics Anonymous may have a contact. If not, contact the NA World Service Office, 16155 Wyandotte Street, Van Nuys, California 91406.

Alcoholics Anonymous, PO Box 23005, Joubert Park 2044. Tel: 23 7219.

Families Anonymous. In 1985 there were no FA meetings yet in South Africa. For up-to-date information write to Families Anonymous, PO Box 528, Van Nuys, California 91408. If your addict uses alcohol (and most do) you can get help from Al-anon.

Al-anon, PO Box 2077, Johannesburg, Transvaal 2000. Tel: 011 29 6696.

Other agencies

South African National Council on Alcoholism and Drug Dependence, Happiness House, corner Loveday and Wolmarans Street, Johannesburg 2001. Tel: 011 725–5810.

APPENDIX 3

Help with Specific Problems

We have listed names and addresses of organisations which may help with specific problems. But do not expect them to understand chemical dependence. Outside counsellors, ignorant of the problem, have been known to suggest to AA members that they are 'cured' or do not need AA. Ignore their advice when it conflicts with AA and NA teaching.

We have listed some campaigning organisations, because many of these have useful advice and services. Campaigners often include individuals who are full of 'righteous anger': remember that recovering addicts and alcoholics cannot afford anger, no matter how righteous the cause.

If you want advice about something which doesn't seem to be listed here, the reference section of your local library can probably help. Librarians are geared to finding out information for people. It would also be worth trying your local Citizens Advice Bureau, or even the local radio station, if the library can't help. If you are writing to any of the organisations listed below, remember to include a stamped and addressed envelope for their reply. This helps the many voluntary organisations who are short of cash.

Alternative medicine and relaxation

Acupuncture: the ancient Chinese system of medicine which works by applying hair-thin needles to specific points. British Acupuncture Association, 34 Alderney Street, London SW1V 4EU. Tel: 01–834 1012. Will supply a list of acupuncturists.

Alexander Technique: a method of re-learning posture so as to balance the body, and in particular the spine, in the right position. Society of Teachers of the Alexander Technique: 10 London House, 266 Fulham Road, London SW10 9EL. Tel: 01–351 0828.

Chiropractic: manipulation of the spine so as to realign the body in the right position. The British Chiropractic Association, 5 First Avenue, Chelmsford, Essex CM1 1RX. Tel: 0245 358487.

Hypnotherapy: hypnosis to stop smoking, help pain, etc. British Society of Medical and Dental Hypnotherapists, 42 Links Road, Ashtead, Surrey, KT21 2HJ. Will supply list of local practitioners, all qualified doctors or dentists.

Naturopathy: a combination of diet, rest, exercise and water treatments to help the body heal itself. British Naturopathic and Osteopathy Association, 6 Netherhall Gardens, London NW3. Tel: 01–435 7830.

Osteopathy: manipulation of the spine and joints to realign the body in the correct position. Usually gentler than chiropractic. Osteopaths General Council and Register, 1 Suffolk Street, London SW1Y 4HG. Tel: 01–839 2060.

Relaxation: Relaxation for Living, 29 Burwood Park Road, Walton on Thames, Surrey KT12 5LH. Relaxation classes throughout England, cassettes, leaflets and correspondence course.

Yoga: Yoga for Health Foundation, Ickwell Bury, Ickwell, Northill, Near Biggleswade, Bedfordshire SG18 9EF. Tel: 076 727 271.

Bereavement

Compassionate Friends, 6 Denmark Street, Bristol BS1 5DQ. Tel: 0272 292778. An organisation to help parents who lose a child of any age for any reason.

Cruse, the National Organisation for the Widowed and their Children, 126 Sheen Road, Richmond, Surrey TW9 1UR. Tel: 01–940 4818/9047.

Foundation for the Study of Infant Deaths. Tel: 01–235 1721 or 01–245 9421. Personal support for parents who have lost babies in cot deaths.

The Miscarriage Association, 19 Stoneybrook Close, West Bretton, Wakefield, West Yorkshire WF4 4TP. Tel: 092 485 515. Local groups give support for women who have had a miscarriage.

National Association for Widows, c/o Stafford District Voluntary Service Centre, Chell Road, Stafford ST16 2QA. Tel: 0785 45465. At the same address is the Widow's Advisory Trust, which gives help to widows with problems. Tel: 0785 58946.

Stillbirth and Neonatal Death Society, Argyle House, 29–31 Euston Road, London NW1 2FD. Tel: 01–833 2851. Support groups for parents who have lost a baby.

Relationships, sex and gender

Adult Children of Alcoholics. Some Al-anon groups are largely made up of adult children of alcoholics. Al-anon family groups, 41 Dover Street, London SE1. Tel: 01–403 0888.

Catholic Marriage Advisory Council, 15 Lansdowne Road, Holland Park, London W11 3AJ. Tel: 01–727 0141. Advises Catholics with marriage difficulties and helps with natural family planning.

Child, Farthings, Gaunts Road, Pawlet, Near Bridgwater, Somerset. Tel: 0278 683595. Self-help for couples with infertility difficulties.

Gay Switchboard. Tel: 01–837 7234. A 24-hour confidential information and advice service for homosexual men and women. The switchboard is very busy, so you may have to keep trying. If you live in a major city outside London, it may have its own gay switchboard. Look in the phone book under 'Gay'.

Gingerbread, 35 Wellington Street, London WC2. Tel: 01–240 0953. Self-help groups for one-parent families.

Incest Crisis Line, 32 Newbury Close, Northolt, Middlesex UB5 4JF. Tel: 01–422 5100 (Richard) or 01–890 4732 (Shirley). They will help with current incest problems or with the problems of those who in the past were incest victims or victims of sexual abuse. There is a network of contacts and counsellors can be recommended.

Lesbian Line. Tel: 01–251 6911. Help and advice for homosexual women.

London Friend, 274 Upper Street, London N1. Tel: 01–359 7371. Counselling for gay men and women.

National Association for the Childless, 318 Summer Lane, Birmingham B19 3RL. Tel: 021–359 4887.

National Council for One-parent Families, 255 Kentish Town Road, London NW5 2LX. Tel: 01–267 1361. Gives information and advice to one-parent families and campaigns on their behalf.

National Marriage Guidance Council, Herbert Gray College, Little Church Street, Rugby, Warwickshire, CV21 3AP. Tel: 0788 73241. Counsels people about their relationships, including non-married and gay couples. Look in your local phone directory under 'Marriage Guidance' for your local branch.

Parents Anonymous, 6–9 Manor Gardens, London N7. Tel: 01–263 8919 (for parents in difficulties) or 01–263 5672 (office). Despite its similar name, this is not a Twelve-Step organisation. It offers help for parents who are worried that they may abuse their children.

Parents Enquiry, 16 Honley Road, London SE6. Tel: 01–698 1815. Counselling for gay teenagers and their families.

Rape Crisis Centre, PO Box 69, London WC1X 9NJ. Tel: 01–837 1600 (24-hour answering service; switchboard manned 10.00 a.m. to 6.00 p.m.; answering machine gives numbers to ring after those hours) or 01–278 3956 (office). The Centre will help women who have been raped or sexually abused in the past, as well as those with current problems.

TV/TS Line. Tel: 01–359 4898. Help for transvestites, transexuals and their relatives.

Women's Aid Federation, 52–54 Featherstone Street, London EC1Y 8RY. Tel: 01–251 6537 (London) or 01–831 8581 (national office). Helps battered women and their children with advice, counselling and refuge. You may find a branch in your local phone directory.

Other problems

AIDS Helpline, Terence Higgins Trust, BN AIDS, WC1N 3XX. Tel: 01–833 2971. Help and advice about AIDS.

Anorexic Aid, The Priory Centre, 11 Priory Road, High Wycombe, Buckinghamshire. Advice and information. Groups run by ex-sufferers.

Association for Postnatal Illness, 7 Gowan Avenue, London SW6 6RH. Support for others who have suffered postnatal depression.

Back Pain Association, 31–33 Park Road, Teddington, Middlesex. Tel: 01–977 5474. Leaflets, books and local branches.

Bacup, British Association of Cancer United Patients, 121–123 Charterhouse Street, London EC1M 6AA. Tel: 01–608 1661. Information about cancer for patients, families and friends.

Foresight, The Old Vicarage, Church Lane, Witley, Godalming, Surrey GU8 5PN. Helps with pre-conception planning and advises on the best way to conceive a healthy child.

Gamblers Anonymous, 17–23 Blantyre Street, London SW10. Tel: 01–352 3060. A Twelve-Step programme for those who gamble compulsively. For partners and friends of gamblers, there is Gam-Anon at the same address and phone number. Look in the local phone book to see if a local GA number is listed.

Mastectomy Association, 26 Harrison Street, off Gray's Inn Road, London WC1H 8JG. Tel: 01–837 0908. Practical advice and help from women who have had mastectomies.

National Childbirth Trust, 9 Queensborough Terrace, London W2 3TB. Tel: 01–221 3833. Antenatal and postnatal courses. Leaflets on relaxation techniques.

Overeaters Anonymous, Manor Gardens Centre, 6–9 Manor Gardens, London N7 6LA. Tel: 01–868 4109. A Twelve-Step programme for people with overeating problems.

Samaritans, 17 Uxbridge, Slough, Berkshire SL1 1SN. Tel: 07533–2713. For the Samaritan phone service in your area look in the local phone book. If it's late at night, you don't know whom to ring, and you feel desperate, the Samaritans are there to talk to you. They help those who feel that life is getting too much to bear and also can help relatives of those who have committed suicide.

Tranx, Tranquilliser Recovery and New Existence, 17 Peel Road, Harrow, Middlesex HA3 7QX. Tel: 01–427 2065. Help and advice for those who may be dependent on tranquillisers and sleeping pills. May help you find a local self-help group. Also look in your local phone book under 'Tranx' or 'Tranquilliser' for other groups.

Recommended Reading

AA and NA books

Alcoholics Anonymous: The so-called 'Big Book' written by the first hundred founders of AA, and published by AA.
Twelve Steps and Twelve Traditions. How members of AA recover and how the society functions, published by AA. Write to the AA national office (address in Appendix 2) for a literature order form.

Narcotics Anonymous. Written by the members of NA and published by NA. Write to the NA national office or to the World Service office (addresses in Appendix 2) for a literature order form.

Alateen: Hope for Children of Alcoholics. Published by Al-anon. Write to the Al-anon national office (address in Appendix 2) for a literature order form.

The Dilemma of the Alcoholic Marriage. Published by Al-anon. Write to the Al-anon national office (address in Appendix 2) for a literature order form.

Other books

Bethune, Helen, *Off the Hook: Coping with Addiction*, Methuen, London 1985.

Cutland, Liz, *Kick Heroin*, Gateway Books, London 1985.

James and Joyce Ditzler, with Celia Haddon, *Coming Off Drugs*, Macmillan, London, 1986.

Gold, Mark S., *800-Cocaine*, Bantam Books, New York, 1984.

Haddon, Celia, *Women and Tranquillisers*, Sheldon Press, London, 1984.

*Hafen, Brent Q., and Fransden, Kathryn J., *Marijuana: Facts, Figures and Information for the 1980s*, Hazelden, Center City, Minnesota, 1980.

*Hafner, A. Jack, *It's Not as Bad as You Think: Coping with Upset Feelings*, Hazelden, Center City, Minnesota, 1981.

*Kurtz, Ernest, *Not God: A History of Alcoholics Anonymous*, Hazelden, Center City, Minnesota, 1979.

**Maxwell, Ruth, *The Booze Battle*, Ballantine, New York, 1976.

**Rice Drews, Toby, *Getting Them Sober, Vols. 1 and 2*, Bridge Publishing, South Plainfield, New Jersey, 1980, 1983.

*Van Almen, W. J., *500 Drugs the Alcoholic Should Avoid*, Hazelden, Center City, Minnesota, 1983.

Young, Howard, S., *A Rational Counselling Primer*, Institute for Rational-Emotive Therapy, New York, 1974.

*Books can be ordered direct from Hazelden Educational Services, Box 176, Center City, Mn 55012. Tel: 612–257–4010. You can pay by international money order or by international credit card.

**A wide variety of books on alcoholism, including the Hazelden publications, is stocked by A. J. Stoyel, 329 Addiscombe Road, Croydon, Surrey.

Index

aches, 73

acupuncture, 156

Adult Children of Alcoholics (ACA), 141, 157

affection, 35

agitation, 75

AIDS, 158

Al-anon, 28, 34, 35, 46, 102, 141; address, 149; joining, 50–1

Alateen, 34, 35, 141; address, 149

alcohol: absorption rates, 16; definition, 15–16; as a depressant, 19–20; duration in the bloodstream, 16; emotional harm, 21–2; physical harm, 16–21; tolerance, 11

alcoholic cardiomyopathy, 18

alcoholic polyneuropathy, 20

alcoholics: appearance, 57; and children, 29–46; damage to, 15–22; deciding to stop, 45; definition, 10; illness and, 119–20; numbers of, 10; potential, 11; self-analysis, 61–5; suffering the consequences, 46; the sufferers, 11–12; teenage, 12–15

Alcoholics Anonymous (AA), 6, 14, 72, 74, 103, 104, 129, 142–3, 144–5; address, 149; difficulties with, 95–6; doing it your way, 96; finding partners, 119; getting involved in, 94; HALT, 81–2; help from, 69–70; importance in recovery, 77–78; meetings, 69, 77; phoning, 77–8, 83; in prison, 140; professional helpers and, 139–40; publications, 160; relapses, 89; Serenity Prayer, 83; sexual problems, 115; sponsors, 95–6; trust in, 99; Twelve Steps, 93–6, 118, 147–8

alcoholism: case studies, 3–6, 12–14, 25–7, 31–2, 34, 45–6, 61–2, 69–70, 91, 102–5, 108–10; as a chemical addiction, 60; costs, 10; as a disease, 14–15, 16–21; early symptoms, 17, 134–5; harm caused by, 7–37; hereditary, 16; myths, 9–10, 16–17; recognising, 58–60, 134–6; scale of the problem, 10–12; sexual behaviour and, 114–18; the sufferers, 11; tell-tale signs of, 40–1, 134–6; as a treatable illness, 39

Alexander technique, 156

alternative medicine, 120; addresses, 156

Andrew, 25–6

anger, 22, 81–2; women alcoholics, 104–14

162